# Weight Watchers™

# FOUR SEASONS
# COOKBOOK

# Weight Watchers™

# FOUR SEASONS
# COOKBOOK

◆

## WENDY GODFREY

### A MONTH-BY-MONTH GUIDE TO HEALTHY EATING

SIMON & SCHUSTER
A VIACOM COMPANY

First published in Great Britain by Simon & Schuster, 1997
A Viacom Company

Copyright © 1997, Weight Watchers (UK) Ltd

Simon & Schuster Ltd
West Garden Place
Kendal Street
London W2 2AQ

First published 1997

Weight Watchers and 1,2,3 Success are Trademarks of Weight Watchers International Inc.
and used under its control by Weight Watchers (U.K.) Ltd.

Design: Jane Humphrey
Typesetting: Stylize
Photography: Steve Baxter
Styling: Sue Russell
Food preparation: Jane Stevenson

Weight Watchers Publications Executive: Juliet Hudson
Weight Watchers Publications Assistant: Celia Whiston

ISBN 0 68481 783 7

Printed and bound in Italy by Printer Trento

Pictured on the front cover:
*Lemon Cheesecake (page 71); Kissel (page 120); Chicory Salad (page 13);*
*Warm Beef and Potato Salad (page 98); and Spring Vegetable Pasta (page 82).*

*Recipe notes:*
Egg size is medium, unless otherwise stated.
Vegetables are medium-sized, unless otherwise stated.
The Points and Calorie values are for the main recipes only;
remember to add extra Points or Calories for the accompaniments.
1 tablespoon = 15 ml; 1 teaspoon = 5 ml.
Dried herbs can be substituted for fresh ones, but the flavour may not always be as good.
Halve the fresh herb quantity stated in the recipe.

*Vegetarian recipes:*
Ⓥ shows the recipe is suitable for vegetarians.

# Contents

◆

# *Introduction*

♦

Welcome to the **Four Seasons Cookbook**, Weight Watchers' beautiful new book, which is packed with delicious recipes to fit into your diet. Designed to help you make the best use of fresh, seasonal ingredients, these recipes can assist you to lose weight, either as part of a Calorie-controlled diet, or through the Weight Watchers Programme. You'll soon understand why healthy eating can be so enjoyable – these recipes will become firm favourites with family and friends alike.

The most obvious advantage of cooking and eating foods in season is flavour – a must for anyone who truly enjoys food! And, better yet, fresh flavour tends to mean low prices. Although ever-expanding world markets mean that we can enjoy fresh summer fruits in January, half the pleasure of devouring strawberries and cream is found in eating them in the garden on a sunny June afternoon – knowing that their season is short-lived increases the enjoyment. Forced fruits and vegetables, or those which have been picked before their time in order to survive the long journey to our supermarkets, seldom have the intensity of flavour found in seasonal produce. Think of the creamy, golden taste of Jersey new potatoes in spring – and compare it to the tasteless (and expensive) little tubers found in the supermarkets in November to see what I mean. Of course, many of the fruits and vegetables we take for granted are imported all year round. Even during a record-breaking heat-wave summer, you're unlikely to find a British-grown banana or grapefruit at the supermarket! However, even these familiar imports have their seasonal peaks. Citrus fruits such as oranges, grapefruit and lemons are best in January and February; and although plum tomatoes, sweet peppers and artichokes can be bought throughout the winter months (thanks to Dutch greenhouses), the true flavours of these Mediterranean vegetables are found only in the summer produce which has ripened naturally under sunny southern skies.

Although we don't think of meat and fish in seasonal terms the way we do vegetables, they are much better value at certain times of the year. There is good reason why so many of us celebrate Easter Sunday with a roast leg of lamb at lunch – British spring lamb is like nothing else. Our cooking methods also reflect the different seasons' natural offerings. Winter is the time to enjoy the warmth of your kitchen and serve stews and slow-simmered casseroles which bring out the best in more mature, tougher joints of meat. Spring and summer are for flash-grilling and barbecuing tender young fillets – and spending as little time as possible over a hot stove! Many locally caught fish are at their best and least expensive during autumn, as the waters cool and the catches increase in size and variety. Native shellfish such as oysters, mussels and cockles are also cheaper and tastier from September through to spring.

Seasonal foods are not only full of flavour and good value for money, but they are a great way to encourage healthy eating. Fresh foods have a high nutritional content and their natural good flavours don't need masking with Calorie-laden or high-fat dressings and sauces. You'll also find that by eating 'seasonally' you'll end up enjoying more fresh fruits and vegetables.

The **Four Seasons Cookbook** is designed to help you choose healthy, seasonal foods all year long. All of the recipes give Calories per serving as well as Points per serving and Total Points per recipe. We've even included four seasonal menu plans which show you how you can fit some of these recipes into your day using only 20 Points (the number of Points suggested for women between 10 and 12 stone). If you weigh under 10 stone we suggest that you start each day with 18 Points. If you weigh more than 12 stone increase your daily Points as follows:

*women who weigh*

*12–14 stone...........................................an extra 2 Points*

*14–16 stone............................................an extra 4 Points*

*more than 16 stone.................................an extra 6 Points*

*and men who weigh*

*under 10 stone.......................................an extra 4 Points*

*10–12 stone............................................an extra 6 Points*

*12–14 stone............................................an extra 8 Points*

*14–16 stone.........................................an extra 10 Points*

*more than 16 stone..............................an extra 12 Points*

*These Points can also be spent on treats or snacks*

*With Weight Watchers **1,2,3 Success™** Programme if you exercise you can earn bonus Points. So if you have spent all your Points or eaten too many Points all is not lost! A brisk half-hour walk will earn you an extra 3 Points, half an hour gardening is worth 2 Points and a half-hour jog is worth 4 Points. Limit the number of bonus Points you spend on food to 12 per week. Adding exercise to a sensible diet will also mean that you tone up as you lose weight. You'll end up slim and fit!*

*Do remember that, in this book, the Points per serving and Total Points per recipe do not always include serving suggestions. Many of the recipes and photographs suggest accompaniments – so remember to calculate extra Points for additional salads, vegetables, breads, rice or pasta, etc. As no foods are forbidden on the Weight Watchers Programme, you can enjoy all your favourite foods – as long as you count the Points!*

*For more details about the **1,2,3 Success™** Programme and Weight Watchers Meetings phone 01628 777077.*

Whether it's spring, summer, autumn or winter when you first open this book, you'll be sure to enjoy many days ahead of happy and healthy cooking and eating – Weight Watchers style.

# January

Not surprisingly, this is the busiest month for Weight Watchers, when many people decide to seek help with their weight-loss goals. It is a good time for everybody to resolve to eat more healthily and to begin shedding any extra pounds, ready for warmer weather. It is also a difficult time for many, as eating can be such a comfort when the weather is really cold and the sun disappears for weeks on end. However, you can enjoy healthy and satisfying foods and still stick to your diet. The recipes in this chapter are sure to provide satisfaction.

Root vegetables are at their best this time of year – try the Parsnip, Potato and Sausage Hot-Pot (page 18), and it's a good time to make thick soups like Lentil and Bacon Soup (page 11), and warming casseroles such as Paprika Chicken (page 17).

Citrus fruits should be at their least expensive now, so do take advantage of the taste of Florida sunshine that an orange or grapefruit can bring to your morning. Easy-peel satsumas or clementines are a quick and tasty low-Point way to finish a meal, or you could make a Fresh Citrus and Rosewater Jelly (page 22) to end a special dinner. I've also included a few recipes which resonate with the echo of Christmas delicacies, such as the Stuffed Pork Fillet (page 16), which has a delicious filling of pickled walnuts and olives.

LENTIL AND BACON SOUP *(page 11)*
STUFFED PORK FILLET *(page 16)*
FRESH CITRUS AND ROSEWATER JELLY *(page 22)*

# FRUITED PORRIDGE

◆

*Serves 1 ◆ Preparation time 5 minutes ◆ Cooking time 5 minutes ◆ Freezing not recommended*
*Hot instant oat cereal provides an excellent start for a cold day. Although oats are a valuable*
*source of starchy food, porridge on its own can be rather bland. This fruity version tastes great.*

Calories per serving: 415
Points per serving: 6½
Ⓥ

*4 tablespoons instant oat cereal*

*a little hot skimmed milk, to mix*

*artificial sweetener, to taste*

*1 small banana, sliced*

*30 g (1 oz) chopped dates*

*1 orange, peeled and segmented*
   *(see below)*

**1** Make the cereal with the hot milk, according to the packet instructions, and add some artificial sweetener, if you like.
**2** Stir in the fruits and enjoy.

**COOK'S NOTE:** Porridge isn't only for winter – try it in the summer with soft fruits, peaches, nectarines or apricots; and in the autumn with plums or blackberries and apple. For extra richness at any time of the year, add a small tub of low-fat yogurt, but don't forget to add the extra Points.

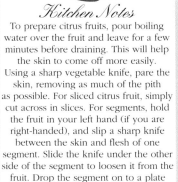

*Kitchen Notes*

To prepare citrus fruits, pour boiling water over the fruit and leave for a few minutes before draining. This will help the skin to come off more easily. Using a sharp vegetable knife, pare the skin, removing as much of the pith as possible. For sliced citrus fruit, simply cut across in slices. For segments, hold the fruit in your left hand (if you are right-handed), and slip a sharp knife between the skin and flesh of one segment. Slide the knife under the other side of the segment to loosen it from the fruit. Drop the segment on to a plate and then repeat round the fruit, squeezing the juice out before discarding the membranes.

◆

# SMOKED MACKEREL PÂTÉ

◆

*Serves 4 ◆ Preparation time 10 minutes ◆ Freezing recommended*
*Oily fish is very good for you because of the omega-3 fatty acids it contains.*
*These fish include mackerel, kippers, herrings and sardines, which are also among the least*
*expensive of fish and have a wonderful flavour. Don't be tempted to put butter or*
*spread on the toast when you eat this pâté – it doesn't need it.*

Calories per serving: 105
Points per serving: 4
Total Points per recipe: 16

*220 g packet of smoked mackerel*
*  fillets with black pepper*
*grated zest and juice of 1 lemon*
*2 tablespoons chopped fresh parsley*
*250 g tub of Quark*

1  Remove the skin from the mackerel and flake the flesh into a basin.
2  Add the grated lemon zest and juice, the parsley and the Quark.
3  Beat together well and transfer to a serving dish.
4  Chill until ready to serve.

# LENTIL AND BACON SOUP

◆

*Serves 4 ◆ Preparation time 10 minutes ◆ Cooking time 30 minutes ◆ Freezing recommended*
*Not only will this soup warm you up, but its high fibre content makes it very satisfying.*

Calories per serving: 180
Points per serving: 3½
Total Points per recipe: 14

*1 tablespoon vegetable oil*
*1 onion, chopped*
*2 garlic cloves, chopped finely*
*2 rashers of lean bacon*
*1 teaspoon dried mixed herbs*
*3 carrots, sliced thinly*
*2 celery sticks, sliced*
*90 g (3 oz) red lentils*
*900 ml (1½ pints) vegetable stock*
*1 tablespoon chopped fresh parsley*
*salt and freshly ground black pepper*

1  Heat the oil in a pan and cook the onion and garlic for 3 minutes.
2  Remove the fat from the bacon and chop the bacon finely (discard the fat). Add the bacon and herbs to the pan, and cook for 5 minutes more.
3  Add the carrots, celery, lentils and stock. Bring to the boil, and then simmer for 20 minutes, or until the lentils are soft.
4  Stir in the parsley, season to taste and serve.

# RED PEPPER SOUP

*Serves 4 ♦ Preparation time 10 minutes ♦ Cooking time 30 minutes ♦ Freezing recommended*
*The brilliant red colour of this soup is enough to warm you. I have used prepared red peppers*
*(sometimes called pimentos) which come in jars or cans. You could also use fresh peppers*
*which, although taking longer to prepare, will give a better flavour.*
*See the note on page 133 on preparing peppers.*

Calories per serving: 170
Points per serving: 0
Total Points per recipe: 0

*1 onion, chopped finely*
*2 garlic cloves, crushed*
*600 ml (1 pint) vegetable stock*
*2 teaspoons paprika*
*400 g can or jar of red peppers*
*400 g can of chopped tomatoes*
*1 tablespoon tomato purée*
*1 tablespoon Worcestershire sauce*
*salt and freshly ground black pepper*

**1** Put the onion and garlic in a pan with enough stock just to cover. Add the paprika and simmer for 5 minutes, until the onion has softened.

**2** Add the remaining ingredients apart from seasoning. Bring to the boil, and then reduce the heat and simmer for 20–25 minutes.

**3** Either sieve, liquidise or whizz the soup in a processor. Season to taste, reheat and serve with warm bread.

*Slim Tips*
Keep a polythene bag or plastic box of
vegetable strips in the refrigerator.
When hunger pangs strike, you'll have
something healthy on hand to nibble on
which has no Points.
♦

# AVOCADO AND HAM SALAD

◆

*Serves 2 ◆ Preparation time 10 minutes ◆ Freezing not recommended*
*Various types of ham can be used in this salad. Whether you use ordinary slices from a packet,*
*or one of the Italian or Spanish cured hams, make sure you remove any visible fat.*

Calories per serving: 125
Points per serving: 2
Total Points per recipe: 4

*½ ripe avocado, peeled and cubed*

*1 tablespoon of lemon juice*

*2 thin slices of ham, cut in strips*

*2 bowl-shaped lettuce leaves*

*6 sprigs of watercress*

**FOR THE DRESSING:**

*2 tablespoons tomato juice*

*1 teaspoon lemon juice*

*2 teaspoons olive oil*

*salt and freshly ground black pepper*

**1**  Toss the avocado with the lemon juice. Mix with the ham and divide between the two lettuce 'bowls'. Garnish with watercress.

**2**  Make the dressing by whisking together all the ingredients, and then pour it over the salad and serve.

# CHICORY SALAD

◆

*Serves 2 ◆ Preparation time 10 minutes ◆ Freezing not recommended*
*The bitter flavour of this salad vegetable blends well with oranges, which are at their best at this*
*time of year. Serve with some toasted olive ciabatta bread.*

Calories per serving: 55
Points per serving: ½
Total Points per recipe: 1
Ⓥ

*1 head of chicory, leaves separated*

*1 orange, peeled and sliced*
  *(see page 10)*

*6 stoned black olives*

*6 sprigs of watercress*

*2 tablespoons low-fat salad dressing*

**1**  Arrange the chicory, orange, olives and watercress on two plates.

**2**  Spoon the dressing over, with any orange juice from the slices.

# COD WITH CRUMBLE TOPPING

◆

*Serves 1 ◆ Preparation time 10 minutes ◆ Cooking time 8 minutes ◆ Freezing not recommended*
*Freshly grilled cod is quite delicious – a far cry from fish in batter. The crumble topping adds*
*a crunchy texture to the fish. Serve it with Chicory Salad (page 13).*

Calories per serving: 150
Points per serving: 3

*90 g (3 oz) piece of cod fillet,*
*    skinned*
*1 teaspoon groundnut oil*
*1 tablespoon oatmeal or dried*
*    breadcrumbs*
*1 tablespoon chopped fresh parsley*
*grated zest and juice of 1 lemon*
*salt and freshly ground black pepper*

**1**  Brush the cod fillet on both sides with the oil.

**2**  Mix together the oatmeal or breadcrumbs, parsley, lemon zest
and seasoning.

**3**  Press the mixture on to both sides of the cod.

**4**  Heat a non-stick frying-pan and cook the cod for 4 minutes on each
side, or grill if you prefer.

**5**  Sprinkle with the lemon juice just before serving.

CHICORY SALAD *(page 13)*
COD WITH CRUMBLE TOPPING

# STUFFED PORK FILLET

♦

*Serves 4 ♦ Preparation time 10 minutes ♦ Cooking time 1 hour ♦ Freezing recommended*
*Pork is low in fat, and this cut is leaner than most. You could use chicken breasts if you prefer.*
*You may well have pickled walnuts left over from Christmas*
*and this is a good way to use them up.*

Calories per serving: 250
Points per serving: 6½
Total Points per recipe: 26

*480 g (1 lb) pork fillet*

*4 pickled walnuts*

*8 stoned olives*

*1 red pepper, de-seeded*

*120 g (4 oz) mushrooms*

*2 garlic cloves*

*4 teaspoons vegetable oil*

*1 tablespoon chopped fresh parsley*

*300 ml (½ pint) stock or white wine*
*   or a mixture of both*

*salt and freshly ground black pepper*

**1**   Make an incision lengthways along the fillet, but not all the way through. Open it out like a book, and beat between two pieces of cling film, using a rolling pin or mallet. This will render the meat quite thin.

**2**   Chop together the walnuts or prunes, olives, pepper, mushrooms and garlic.

**3**   Heat two teaspoons of the oil in a pan and fry the chopped filling for 5 minutes.

**4**   Remove from the heat and add the parsley and seasoning.

**5**   Spread the filling over the fillet, leaving a 2.5 cm (1-inch) border.

**6**   Roll up the meat and fasten with string, skewers or cocktail sticks.

**7**   Heat the remaining oil in a flameproof casserole and brown the fillet all over until sealed.

**8**   Add the stock or wine, bring to the boil, and then cover and simmer for 1 hour.

**9**   Remove the meat from the casserole and let rest for 5–10 minutes, and then remove the string or skewers and slice to serve.

**10**   Boil the juices until slightly reduced, and serve with the sliced meat.

**VARIATION:** Use 4 ready-to-eat prunes instead of the walnuts. This will decrease the Points per serving to 6.

# PAPRIKA CHICKEN

◆

*Serves 2 ◆ Preparation time 10 minutes ◆ Cooking time 30 minutes ◆ Freezing recommended*
*This casserole has a real Hungarian flavour, and is very similar to a goulash.*
*As most of the fat in poultry is in and just under the skin, choose skinless chicken for this recipe.*
*Serve with boiled rice or noodles and a green vegetable or salad.*

Calories per serving: 240
Points per serving: 3½
Total Points per recipe: 7

*2 skinless chicken thighs or 4*
*    skinless drumsticks*
*15 g (½ oz) flour, seasoned with*
*    salt, pepper and 2 teaspoons of*
*    paprika*
*1 tablespoon vegetable oil*
*1 onion, chopped*
*150 ml (¼ pint) chicken stock*
*60 g (2 oz) mushrooms, wiped*
*    and sliced*
*2 tomatoes, quartered*
*1 tablespoon tomato purée*
*salt and freshly ground black pepper*

**1**  Coat the chicken pieces in the seasoned flour (see page 153).

**2**  Heat the oil in a frying-pan or flameproof casserole, and cook the onion until soft.

**3**  Add the chicken pieces with any leftover coating. Cook until browned all over.

**4**  Stir in the chicken stock and bring to the boil.

**5**  Reduce the heat, add the mushrooms, tomatoes and tomato purée. Cover and simmer for 25 minutes, adding a little boiling water if the sauce gets too thick.

**6**  Season to taste and serve hot.

# CHRYSANTHEMUM ONIONS

◆

*Serves 1 ◆ Preparation time 5 minutes ◆ Cooking time 40 minutes ◆ Freezing recommended*
*We tend to treat onions as simply a flavouring ingredient, but they can make a good vegetable*
*dish in their own right. Serve this with a tomato sauce (page 49).*

Calories per serving: 195
Points per serving: 2½
Ⓥ

2 onions
150 ml (¼ pint) vegetable stock
15 g (½ oz) butter or margarine,
    melted
salt and freshly ground black pepper

**1**  Preheat the oven to Gas Mark 7/220°C/425°F.

**2**  Trim the stem end of the onions and remove the brown skin. Leave the root intact, but trim so that the onion can balance on its own.

**3**  Cut the onions right down to the root in 5 mm (¼-inch) slices one way, and then across the other way.

**4**  Put the onions in an ovenproof dish or tin and pour the stock over. Brush the tops with the butter or margarine.

**5**  Season and cover with kitchen foil. Bake for 40 minutes, until the onions are soft and the tips of the 'petals' are golden brown.

# PARSNIP, POTATO AND SAUSAGE HOT-POT

◆

*Serves 4 ◆ Preparation time 15 minutes ◆ Cooking time 1 hour ◆ Freezing not recommended*
*Root vegetables are really inexpensive in winter, and add a distinctive flavour to any dish.*

Calories per serving: 390
Points per serving: 7
Total Points per recipe: 28

4 parsnips, peeled and sliced
1 onion, sliced
480 g (1 lb) half-fat sausages,
    skinned
400 g can of chopped tomatoes
2 teaspoons dried sage
480 g (1 lb) potatoes, peeled
    and sliced
1 tablespoon vegetable oil
salt and freshly ground black pepper

**1**  Preheat the oven to Gas Mark 5/190°C/375°F.

**2**  Boil the parsnips and onion for 15 minutes in just enough water to cover. Drain and reserve the cooking water, and transfer the vegetables to an ovenproof dish.

**3**  Arrange the sausages on top and season well.

**4**  Pour the tomatoes over and sprinkle with the sage. Season again.

**5**  Arrange the potato slices on top and drizzle with 4 tablespoons of the reserved cooking water.

**6**  Brush the potatoes with oil, and bake on the top shelf of the oven for about 45 minutes, or until the potatoes are browned and crisp.

**VARIATION:** Turnips or swede could be used instead of parsnips. This will be 6 Points per serving.

# RED CABBAGE STIR-FRY

♦

*Serves 2 ♦ Preparation time 10 minutes ♦ Cooking time 10 minutes ♦ Freezing not recommended*
*Red cabbage will turn blue on cooking unless an acidic ingredient is added – in this case,*
*cooking apple and orange juice. This delicious vegetable and fruit stir-fry*
*could be served with grilled meat or fish.*

Calories per serving: 190
Points per serving: 2
Total Points per recipe: 4

*1 tablespoon vegetable oil*

*1 garlic clove, chopped finely*

*2.5 cm (1-inch) piece of fresh root*
  *ginger, peeled and chopped*

*1 red pepper, de-seeded and sliced*

*360 g (12 oz) red cabbage,*
  *quartered, cored and shredded*

*60 g (2 oz) french beans, topped,*
  *tailed and cut in 5 cm (2-inch)*
  *pieces*

*1 cooking apple, peeled, cored*
  *and sliced*

*2 tablespoons orange juice*

*1 teaspoon soy sauce*

*salt and freshly ground black pepper*

**1** Heat the oil in a wok or large frying-pan and gently cook the garlic and ginger for 3 minutes.

**2** Increase the heat and add the red pepper.

**3** Add the cabbage and beans and stir-fry for 5 minutes.

**4** Add the apple, orange juice and soy sauce and cook for 5 minutes more.

**5** Season to taste and serve immediately.

*Kitchen Notes*

Stir-frying is always done over a fierce heat in a pan with steep sides and very little oil. The technique is to stir and toss the ingredients the whole time so that they do not catch on the bottom. Ingredients can be added at different times if one takes longer to cook than others. A non-stick wok is a good investment, and you'll need a draining spoon or wooden spatula for tossing the ingredients.

♦

# SIZZLING BEEF STRIPS

◆

*Serves 4 ◆ Preparation time 15 minutes ◆ Cooking time 5 minutes ◆ Freezing not recommended*
*This Chinese-inspired stir-fry must be served immediately, so that it is still sizzling on the plate.*
*Prepare all the ingredients ahead, and have some steamed*
*or boiled rice ready to serve alongside.*

Calories per serving: 195
Points per serving: 3½
Total Points per recipe: 14

*240 g (8 oz) braising steak*
*1 carrot, peeled and cut in*
   *matchsticks*
*1 celery stick, cut in matchsticks*
*4 spring onions, cut in 2.5 cm*
   *(1-inch) diagonal slices*
*1 tablespoon light soy sauce*
*1 teaspoon Chinese five-spice*
   *powder*
*2 tablespoons cornflour*
*3 tablespoons groundnut or*
   *vegetable oil*

**1** Beat the steak with a rolling pin or meat mallet, to tenderise it. Cut in thin strips.

**2** Mix the beef with the carrot, celery, spring onions, soy sauce and five-spice powder.

**3** Sprinkle with the cornflour and toss to make sure all the ingredients are coated.

**4** Heat the oil in a wok or frying-pan until hot, and stir-fry the strips until crisp and sizzling.

**5** Drain and serve at once.

# FRESH CITRUS AND ROSEWATER JELLY

◆

*Serves 4 ◆ Preparation time 10 minutes + 1¾ hours setting ◆ Freezing not recommended*
*Oranges and rosewater are often combined in Middle Eastern cooking. If you have ever tasted*
*Turkish Delight, you will know the lovely scented flavour of rosewater, which is easily purchased*
*at chemists and larger supermarkets. It is optional, but it does add something special.*
*Make sure you ask for triple-strength rosewater.*

Calories per serving: 80
Points per serving: 1
Total Points per recipe: 4
Ⓥ if using a gelatine substitute

*1 orange, segmented (see page 10),*
*with juice reserved*
*1 grapefruit, segmented, with juice*
*reserved*
*450 ml (¾ pint) freshly squeezed*
*orange juice*
*1 sachet of powdered gelatine*
*1 teaspoon triple-strength rosewater*
*(optional)*

**1**  Arrange the orange and grapefruit segments in the bottom of a jelly mould or basin.

**2**  Make up any reserved juices to 150 ml (¼ pint) with some of the freshly-squeezed orange juice. Heat in a small pan, and then remove from the heat and sprinkle the gelatine over. Stir until dissolved.

**3**  Add the remaining juice and the rosewater, if using, to the gelatine. Add extra rosewater if you want a stronger flavour.

**4**  Pour a thin layer of the liquid jelly over the fruit, and set the mould or basin over a bowl of ice cubes.

**5**  Allow to set – about 15 minutes – and then pour the remaining liquid jelly over and refrigerate for 1½ hours, or until set.

**6**  Dip the mould in a basin of hot water to loosen the jelly, and turn out on a plate.

**7**  If you like, peel thin strips of zest from the orange to decorate the top before serving.

# SULTANA AND SPICE SCONES

◆

*Makes 8 scones* ◆ *Preparation time 10 minutes* ◆ *Cooking time 10 minutes* ◆ *Freezing recommended*
*The smell of baking and the warmth of the oven is very comforting in cold weather.*

Calories per serving: 170
Points per serving: 3
Total Points per recipe: 24

ⓥ

240 g (8 oz) self-raising flour

1 teaspoon ground mixed spice

60 g (2 oz) soft margarine

60 g (2 oz) sultanas

150 ml (¼ pint) skimmed milk, plus
extra, for brushing

**1**  Preheat the oven to Gas Mark 8/230°C/450°F.

**2**  Sieve the flour and spice together into a bowl.

**3**  Rub in the margarine, and then stir in the fruit. Mix together to a soft dough with the milk.

**4**  On a floured surface, shape the dough in a circle about 2 cm (¾ inch) thick.

**5**  Transfer to a greased baking tray and brush with milk.

**6**  Cut through into 8 segments and bake for 8–10 minutes, until risen and golden brown.

**7**  Remove to a wire rack to cool.

**VARIATIONS:** This basic recipe can be altered to taste. Replace the sultanas with half-fat grated cheese and the spice with dried mustard, or simply substitute chopped, stoned dates for the sultanas (the Points will remain the same). Mixed herbs and chopped, drained sun-dried tomatoes make lovely Mediterranean scones.

# February

This is the month of St Valentine, so treat your body as your best-loved friend and be especially kind to your heart by choosing low-Point healthy foods all month long. Many of the recipes in this chapter could be adapted to make a special Valentine's Day meal. Try cutting the Smoked Haddock Fishcakes (page 30) into heart shapes, or arrange the Citrus Platter (page 26) on a pretty pink plate and enjoy a leisurely breakfast in bed.

Root vegetables are still plentiful this month – take advantage of their flavour and economy, and use a wide variety in the Minestrone (page 26) and Winter Vegetable Hot-Pot (page 34). Along with starchy low-fat foods like potatoes, lentils, beans, pasta and rice, root vegetables are a great way to fill and warm yourself during the cold days of winter.

Herring and haddock are also in good supply this month. They contain essential fatty acids and are a valuable source of protein. I've included recipes for both, but you could just as easily enjoy them plainly grilled with a winter salad like the Cauliflower Coleslaw (page 29).

SMOKED HADDOCK FISHCAKES *(page 30)*
CAULIFLOWER COLESLAW *(page 29)*
FLORIDA FLAN *(page 37)*

# CITRUS PLATTER

◆

*Serves 1 ◆ Preparation time 5 minutes ◆ Freezing not recommended*
*Serve this healthy sweet platter for breakfast, or add a scoop of lemon sorbet*
*and enjoy it as a refreshing dessert.*

Calories per serving: 140
Points per serving: 1½
Ⓥ

1 orange
1 pink grapefruit

1  Using a small sharp knife, pare the skin from the fruit (see page 10).
2  Cut the orange across in slices, reserving any juices.
3  Cut the grapefruit into segments, reserving any juices.
4  Arrange the fruit prettily on a plate and drizzle any juices over.

# MINESTRONE

◆

*Serves 4 ◆ Preparation time 15 minutes ◆ Cooking time 30 minutes ◆ Freezing recommended*
*This Italian peasant soup has no pretensions towards haute cuisine, but makes a satisfying and*
*warming light meal or a substantial starter. Use whatever vegetables you have on hand. Serve*
*with Italian ciabatta bread or breadsticks. You could sprinkle the soup with a little grated*
*Parmesan – remember that 1 tablespoon will cost you 1½ Points.*

Calories per serving: 170
Points per serving: 2½
Total Points per recipe: 10

1 tablespoon vegetable oil
1 onion, chopped
2 garlic cloves, sliced
2 rashers of lean bacon
360 g (12 oz) prepared mixed
   vegetables
1.5 litres (2½ pints) hot vegetable
   stock
2 tablespoons tomato purée
1 teaspoon mixed dried herbs
2 bay leaves
60 g (2 oz) pasta shapes or short
   macaroni
salt and freshly ground black pepper

1  Heat the oil in a large pan and fry the onion and garlic with the chopped bacon for 5 minutes, without browning.
2  Prepare the vegetables and cut into 1 cm (½-inch) pieces.
3  Add the vegetables to the pan, cover and cook for 5 minutes.
4  Pour in the hot stock, tomato purée and herbs.
5  Bring to the boil and then cover, reduce the heat, and simmer for 20 minutes.
6  Add the pasta and cook for 10 minutes more.
7  Season to taste, remove the bay leaves and serve.

# PASTRAMI PITTA

◆

*Serves 1 ◆ Preparation time 5 minutes ◆ Freezing not recommended*
*Sandwiches are very popular light meals these days. In this recipe, I've used pitta bread and given*
*some alternative ideas for different fillings and other breads.*

Calories per serving: 250
Points per serving: 3½

*1 wholemeal pitta bread*
*2 crisp lettuce leaves, shredded*
*2 slices of pastrami*
*1 tablespoon prepared salsa*
*30 g (1 oz) bean sprouts*
*freshly ground black pepper*

**1** Cut the pitta in half and ease each half open to fill.

**2** Stuff the lettuce in the bottom of each pocket.

**3** Put the pastrami in next, followed by the salsa and then the
bean sprouts.

**4** Season with pepper and enjoy.

**VARIATIONS:** Use wholemeal muffins, split in half, baps, ciabatta rolls,
or mini french sticks. Fill with lean 'shaved' turkey or chicken mixed
with Quark and chopped fresh herbs, lean ham with mustard and cherry
tomatoes, or tandoori chicken pieces with cucumber and yogurt. (The
Points will vary according to what you choose.)

# CHINESE MUSHROOMS

◆

*Serves 4* ◆ *Preparation time 10 minutes* ◆ *Cooking time 10 minutes + marinating* ◆
*Freezing recommended*

*Lightly cooked mushrooms, served cold, make an excellent lunch. In this recipe I have used oriental flavours and Chinese-style mushrooms. You can use button mushrooms instead, but do try to include a few oyster or shiitake mushrooms, which have lovely deep flavours and a delicate appearance. Serve with crusty bread to mop up the juices.*

Calories per serving: 30
Points per serving: 0
Total Points per recipe: 0

*2 tablespoons lime juice*

*240 g (8 oz) shiitake mushrooms*

*240 g (8 oz) oyster mushrooms*

*1 garlic clove, crushed*

*2.5 cm (1-inch) piece of fresh root
    ginger, peeled and chopped finely*

*¼ teaspoon chilli powder*

*1 teaspoon soy sauce*

*1 teaspoon dry sherry*

*1 teaspoon sesame oil*

**TO GARNISH:**

*2 spring onions, sliced*

*a few fresh coriander leaves*

**1**  Put the lime juice in a small pan and heat with the mushrooms for about 5 minutes.

**2**  Remove the mushrooms with a draining spoon and place in a serving dish.

**3**  Add the remaining ingredients to the cooking liquid and boil briskly for 3 minutes.

**4**  Pour the liquid over the mushrooms and leave to marinate in the liquid until cold.

**5**  Garnish with spring onions and coriander.

*Kitchen Notes*
Don't deprive your family of the occasional Chinese take-away or meal out. Simply steer clear of battered and deep-fried dishes. Choose steamed and stir-fried vegetables instead. Order plenty of steamed rice (not egg-fried).
◆

# LEEKS IN HAM PARCELS

*Serves 2* ♦ *Preparation time 10 minutes* ♦ *Cooking time 20 minutes* ♦
*Freezing recommended without the sauce*

*Leeks are an underrated vegetable. With their oniony flavour and bright green colour, they add a distinctive touch to many winter dishes.*

Calories per serving: 125
Points per serving: 3½
Total Points per recipe: 7

*2 leeks, cleaned and trimmed*

*2 thin slices of lean ham*

*2 teaspoons wholegrain mustard*

*4 tablespoons very-low-fat fromage frais*

*30 g (1 oz) half-fat cheese, grated*

*1 tablespoon dried breadcrumbs*

1  Cut the leeks in half. Cook them in lightly salted boiling water for 10 minutes, until tender but still firm. Drain well.

2  Spread each slice of ham with mustard. Preheat the grill.

3  Divide the cooked leeks between the ham slices and roll them up. Place in a warm ovenproof dish.

4  Spoon the fromage frais over.

5  Mix together the cheese and breadcrumbs and sprinkle over the top.

6  Grill until golden brown and bubbling. Serve immediately.

# CAULIFLOWER COLESLAW

*Serves 2* ♦ *Preparation time 10 minutes* ♦ *Freezing not recommended*
*Coleslaw is one of the most popular side salads, but this coleslaw is a meal in itself.*

Calories per serving: 155
Points per serving: 2½
Total Points per recipe: 5
  if using vegetarian cheese

*120 g (4 oz) cauliflower*

*120 g (4 oz) white cabbage, shredded*

*1 carrot, grated*

*60 g (2 oz) half-fat Cheddar cheese, grated*

*2 tablespoons very-low-fat fromage frais*

*1 tablespoon lemon juice*

*1 teaspoon curry paste (optional)*

*salt and freshly ground black pepper*

*1 tablespoon chopped fresh parsley, to garnish*

1  Cut the cauliflower into tiny florets. Mix together the shredded cabbage, cauliflower, grated carrot and cheese.

2  Stir in the fromage frais, lemon juice and curry paste, if using; season to taste.

3  Transfer to a serving bowl or two individual dishes and sprinkle with parsley before serving.

# ORANGE BAKED PORK

*Serves 4 ♦ Preparation time 5 minutes ♦ Cooking time 30 minutes ♦ Freezing recommended*
*We are used to serving pork with apple sauce, but this citrus-flavoured pork is a real*
*delight. Enjoy this dish with baked potatoes and a green salad.*

Calories per serving: 230
Points per serving: 6
Total Points per recipe: 24

1 tablespoon oil

4 pork steaks

1 onion, sliced thinly

thinly sliced zest and juice of 1 orange

150 ml (¼ pint) unsweetened
   orange juice

1 teaspoon ground cardamom

1 tablespoon chopped fresh chives

salt and freshly ground black pepper

**1**  Heat the oil in a shallow flameproof casserole and brown the steaks and onion.

**2**  Add the orange juices and cardamom to the casserole.

**3**  Bring to the boil, and then cover and reduce the heat. Simmer for 30 minutes.

**4**  Meanwhile, blanch the orange zest and drain (see page 128).

**5**  Season the pan juices, pour over the pork and garnish each steak with the chives and blanched orange zest.

# SMOKED HADDOCK FISHCAKES

*Makes 12 fishcakes ♦ Preparation time 10 minutes ♦ Cooking time 40 minutes ♦*
*Freezing recommended*
*Potatoes don't need lashings of butter and cream when they're mashed.*
*Freeze any leftover fishcakes and serve them for a weekend breakfast.*

Calories per 2-fishcake serving: 140
Points per 2-fishcake serving: 2
Total Points per recipe: 12

720 g (1½ lb) old potatoes

240 g (8 oz) smoked haddock or
   cod fillet

4 tablespoons skimmed milk

1 tablespoon lemon juice

2 tablespoons chopped fresh parsley

1 tablespoon vegetable oil

salt and freshly ground black pepper

**1**  Boil the potatoes in lightly salted water for about 20 minutes.

**2**  At the same time, poach the fish in the skimmed milk on a plate resting over the boiling potatoes. It is cooked when the flesh is firm and opaque.

**3**  Drain the potatoes, reserving some of the cooking water. Mash with the poaching milk from the fish, and then flake the fish and mix it into the mashed potato.

**4**  Beat in the lemon juice and parsley, and season to taste.

**5**  Leave the mixture to cool, and then divide and shape into twelve patties, about 1 cm (½ inch) thick.

**6**  Brush a non-stick frying-pan with the oil, and fry the cakes for 5 minutes on each side. You may need to cook them in two batches.

# HERRING WITH MUSTARD TOPPING

◆

*Serves 1 ◆ Preparation time 5 minutes ◆ Cooking time 8 minutes ◆ Freezing recommended*
*Herring and mackerel are good value at this time of the year, and are very tasty when grilled.*
*Simply multiply the ingredients to make this for more than one person.*
*Ask the fishmonger to fillet the fish for you to save time, or buy fillets from the supermarket.*

Calories per serving: 285
Points per serving: 8

*180 g (6 oz) herring or small*
  *mackerel fillet*
*1 tablespoon wholegrain or French*
  *mustard*
*1 teaspoon lemon juice*
*1 tablespoon dried natural*
  *breadcrumbs*

**FOR THE SAUCE:**

*1 tablespoon very-low-fat fromage*
  *frais*
*1 teaspoon wholegrain or French*
  *mustard*
*salt and freshly ground black pepper*

**1**  Preheat the grill. Rinse the fish and pat dry with kitchen paper.

**2**  Mix together the mustard, lemon juice and breadcrumbs and season well.

**3**  Grill the fish on the skin side for 3 minutes.

**4**  Turn and spread the mustard topping on the flesh side, and then grill for 5 minutes more.

**5**  Meanwhile, blend together the fromage frais and mustard and season to taste.

**6**  Serve the grilled fish with the cold mustard sauce on top.

**VARIATION:** This treatment would work equally well with barbecued trout in the summer.

# CHICKEN WITH CIDER AND FRUIT SAUCE

♦

*Serves 4 ♦ Preparation time 10 minutes ♦ Cooking time 1 hour ♦ Freezing recommended*
*This spicy, fruity dish goes well with vegetables and plain rice or couscous.*

Calories per serving: 265
Points per serving: 5
Total Points per recipe: 20

*4 skinless chicken breasts or thighs*

*1 tablespoon olive oil*

*1 tablespoon lemon juice*

*1 tablespoon Dijon mustard*

*1 cooking apple*

*120 g (4 oz) ready-to-eat dried*
*apricots*

*120 g (4 oz) ready-to-eat prunes*

*240 ml (8 fl oz) dry cider*

*2 teaspoons ground cinnamon*

*salt and freshly ground black pepper*

**1**  Preheat the oven to Gas Mark 4/180°C/350°F.

**2**  Place the chicken portions, bone-side up, in an ovenproof dish or roasting pan.

**3**  Spread with a mixture of oil, lemon juice and mustard.

**4**  Bake for 30 minutes, turning the chicken over half-way through.

**5**  Peel, core and slice the apple. Heat together the apple, apricots, prunes, cider and cinnamon until boiling, and then simmer for 10 minutes.

**6**  Pour the fruit sauce over the chicken and bake for 30 minutes more.

# CHILLI CON CARNE

♦

*Serves 4 ♦ Preparation time 5 minutes ♦ Cooking time 30 minutes ♦ Freezing recommended*
*This Mexican recipe should be fairly hot: regulate this with the amount and strength of chilli*
*powder. The leaner the mince you use, the healthier your chilli will be.*

Calories per serving: 255
Points per serving: 4
Total Points per recipe: 16

*1 tablespoon vegetable oil*

*1 onion, chopped*

*240 g (8 oz) minced beef*

*¼-1 teaspoon chilli powder, to taste*

*1 teaspoon dried mixed herbs*

*432 g can of chilli beans or red*
*kidney beans, drained*

*400 g can of chopped tomatoes*

*salt and freshly ground black pepper*

**1**  Heat the oil and fry the onion for 5 minutes.

**2**  Add the minced beef, chilli powder and herbs.

**3**  Cook until the meat has browned, stirring occasionally to break up the meat.

**4**  Add the beans and tomatoes and cook gently for 30 minutes.

**5**  Season to taste before serving.

WINTER VEGETABLE HOT-POT *(page 34)*
CHICKEN WITH CIDER AND FRUIT SAUCE

# WINTER VEGETABLE HOT-POT

*Serves 4 ♦ Preparation time 10 minutes ♦ Cooking time 1 hour ♦ Freezing recommended*
*You could make an individual hot-pot but, if you are going to heat the oven, you might as well*
*make enough for more than one person, and freeze any leftovers.*

Calories per serving: 325
Points per serving: 4
Total Points per recipe: 16
Ⓥ

*2 onions, sliced*

*2 leeks, cleaned and sliced*

*2 carrots, peeled and cut in*
  *matchsticks*

*1 parsnip, peeled and cubed*

*2 celery sticks, sliced*

*1 small swede, peeled and cubed*

*60 g (2 oz) flour, seasoned*

*600 ml (1 pint) vegetable stock*

*1 teaspoon yeast extract*

*1 tablespoon tomato purée*

*1 teaspoon dried mixed herbs*

*720 g (1½ lb) potatoes, peeled and*
  *sliced thinly*

*1 tablespoon vegetable oil*

*salt and freshly ground black pepper*

**1**  Preheat the oven to Gas Mark 4/180°C/350°F.

**2**  Mix together the prepared vegetables, except for the potatoes, and toss in seasoned flour. Put in an ovenproof dish or casserole.

**3**  Mix together the stock, yeast extract, tomato purée and herbs, and pour over the vegetables.

**4**  Arrange the potato slices on top, overlapping if necessary.

**5**  Brush with the oil and cover before placing in the middle of the oven.

**6**  After 45 minutes, remove the lid and transfer to the top shelf of the oven for about 15 minutes, until the potatoes are crisp and brown.

# LAMB AND LENTILS

◆

*Serves 4 ◆ Preparation time 10 minutes ◆ Cooking time 30 minutes ◆ Freezing recommended*
*Dried lentils do not require soaking nor do they take long to cook. If you prefer, you can use*
*canned lentils, but it is best to use green or Puy lentils. Serve with steamed carrots and broccoli.*

Calories per serving: 510
Points per serving: 8½
Total Points per recipe: 34

*480 g (1 lb) lamb fillet or lean lamb,*
*  cubed*
*1 teaspoon dried rosemary*
*1 tablespoon vegetable oil*
*2 onions, chopped*
*4 garlic cloves, halved*
*2 celery sticks, sliced*
*250 g packet of green or Puy lentils*
*  or 2 × 420 g cans of green lentils,*
*  drained*
*600 ml (1 pint) lamb or chicken*
*  stock*
*1 tablespoon chopped capers*
*salt and freshly ground black pepper*

**1**  Sprinkle the lamb with the rosemary and season well.

**2**  Heat the oil in a flameproof casserole or a heavy-based pan.

**3**  Add the onions, garlic and celery, and cook until beginning to turn brown.

**4**  Add the lamb cubes and fry until the meat is sealed.

**5**  Stir in the dried lentils and mix with the other ingredients.

**6**  Add the stock and capers, bring to the boil, and then lower the heat and simmer for 30 minutes, adding more stock or water if necessary. If using canned lentils, add only 300 ml (½ pint) of stock and add the drained lentils to the pan after the meat has been simmering for 20 minutes.

# RICE PUDDING WITH DRIED FRUITS

◆

*Serves 2 ◆ Preparation time 5 minutes ◆ Cooking time 5 minutes ◆ Freezing not recommended*
*Canned rice puddings make an excellent base for hot or cold desserts, and they are*
*now available in low-fat versions. This pudding is heated through*
*with your choice of high-fibre fruits.*

Calories per serving: 305
Points per serving: 2
Total Points per recipe: 4

400 g can of rice pudding
120 g (4 oz) mixed dried fruits
   (e.g. raisins, sultanas, chopped
   dates, candied peel, ready-to-eat
   apricots, mango slices or apple
   rings)
1 teaspoon ground mixed spice

**1**   Place all the ingredients in a pan and heat slowly, stirring constantly.
Serve hot.

**VARIATION:** Serve this pudding chilled and topped with fresh berries
during the summer months.

# FLORIDA FLAN

♦

*Serves 4 ♦ Preparation time 10 minutes ♦ Cooking time 5 minutes ♦ Freezing not recommended*
*The base for this dessert is a ready-made fatless sponge flan, similar to trifle sponges or a*
*swiss roll. It is livened up with delicious citrus fruits to bring some Florida sunshine*
*into the drab days of February.*

Calories per serving: 165
Points per serving: 2½
Total Points per recipe: 10

*15 cm (6-inch) ready-made*
*sponge flan*
*2 sweet oranges, peeled and*
*segmented (see page 10)*
*2 pink grapefruit, peeled and*
*segmented (see page 10)*
*150 ml (¼ pint) unsweetened*
*orange juice*
*2 teaspoons arrowroot*

**1**  Put the sponge flan on a serving plate.

**2**  Arrange the fruit segments in concentric circles on the flan.

**3**  Add any extra juices to the orange juice and blend with the arrowroot in a small pan.

**4**  Bring to the boil, stirring constantly, and boil for 1 minute, until thickened.

**5**  Pour the thickened juice over the fruit and leave to cool before serving.

# Spring

♦

# MENU PLAN

## MONDAY

### BREAKFAST
1 medium slice honeydew
melon: 1 Point
1 slice toast: 1 Point
1 heaped teaspoon peanut
butter: 1½ Points

♦

### LUNCH
1 small can (300 g/10 oz)
chicken soup: 3 Points
a 5 cm (2-inch) slice
french bread: 1½ Points
1 teaspoon low-fat spread:
½ Point
1 small can (210 g)
raspberries in natural juice:
1 Point

♦

### DINNER
*Spring Vegetable Pasta*
*(page 82):* 4 Points
1 corn on the cob: 1 Point
green salad with
fat-free salad dressing:
0 Points
1 pear: 1 Point

———

### MILK
600 ml (1 pint) skimmed
milk: 2 Points

### TREAT
1 small bag potato crisps:
2½ Points

## TUESDAY

### BREAKFAST
½ grapefruit with granular
artificial sweetener:
½ Point
2 Ryvita: 1 Point
2 teaspoons Marmite:
0 Points

♦

### LUNCH
*Indian Chicken Sandwich*
*(page 77):* 6½ Points
1 small tub low-fat natural
yogurt: 1½ Points
1 small glass fruit juice:
½ Point

♦

### DINNER
2 fish cakes: 3 Points
2 scoops mashed potato:
2 Points
2 tablespoons peas:
1 Point
broccoli and carrots:
0 Points

———

### MILK
300 ml (½ pint) skimmed
milk: 1 Point

### TREAT
1 small slice malt loaf:
1½ Points
1 teaspoon low-fat spread:
½ Point
2 heaped teaspoons jam:
1 Point

## WEDNESDAY

### BREAKFAST
1 crumpet: 1 Point
2 teaspoons low-fat
spread: 1 Point
1 small tub low-fat
natural yogurt:
1½ Points
1 small banana: 1 Point

♦

### LUNCH
2 medium slices honey-
roast ham: 2 Points
salad of tomatoes,
cucumber, lettuce
and cress: 0 Points
2 tablespoons Weight
Watchers from Heinz
Low-fat Mild Mustard
Salad Dressing: ½ Point
1 thick slice bread:
1½ Points
2 teaspoons low-fat
spread: 1 Point

♦

### DINNER
*Chicken Liver and*
*Mangetout Stir-fry*
*(page 66):* 2½ Points
1 medium pitta:
2½ Points
1 large slice fresh
pineapple: ½ Point

———

### MILK
300 ml (½ pint)
skimmed milk: 1 Point

### TREAT
1 jam doughnut:
4 Points

## THURSDAY

BREAKFAST
*Yogurt with Bananas
(page 74):* 5¹/₂ Points

♦

LUNCH
1 hard-boiled egg:
1¹/₂ Points
salad of watercress and
cherry tomatoes with
fat-free salad dressing:
0 Points
1 apple or pear: ¹/₂ Point
1 slice bread: 1 Point
1 teaspoon low-fat spread:
¹/₂ Point

♦

DINNER
2 low-fat chipolatas, grilled
with sliced onions:
2 Points
2 scoops mashed potato:
2 Points
1 small can (205 g) Weight
Watchers from Heinz
Baked Beans: 1¹/₂ Points
*Lemon Cheesecake
(page 71):* 4 Points

─────

MILK
300 ml (¹/₂ pint) skimmed
milk: 1 Point

TREAT
2 rings pineapple in juice:
¹/₂ Point

## FRIDAY

BREAKFAST
1 small glass fruit juice:
¹/₂ Point
1 medium bowl
cornflakes: 1¹/₂ Points
150 ml (¹/₄ pint) skimmed
milk: ¹/₂ Point

♦

LUNCH
*Spanish Omelette
(page 61):* 2¹/₂ Points
tomato and pepper salad:
0 Points

♦

DINNER
1 medium portion chicken
kiev: 8 Points
1 medium baked potato:
2¹/₂ Points
2 tablespoons grated
Cheddar cheese: 2 Points
green salad with fat-free
salad dressing: 0 Points

─────

MILK
450 ml (³/₄ pint) skimmed
milk: 1¹/₂ Points

TREAT
1 small can (210 g/7 oz)
pears in juice: 1 Point

## SATURDAY

BREAKFAST
¹/₂ grapefruit with granular
artificial sweetener:
¹/₂ Point
2 slices low-Calorie bread:
1 Point
2 teaspoons low-fat
spread: 1 Point
2 heaped teaspoons
honey: 1 Point

♦

LUNCH
2 slices toast: 2 Points
1 small can (205 g) Weight
Watchers from Heinz
Spaghetti in Tomato Sauce:
1¹/₂ Points
salad of sliced tomatoes
and cucumber with
fat-free salad dressing:
0 Points
1 small bunch grapes:
1 Point

♦

DINNER
*Cod in a Parcel
(page 80):* 2 Points
3 scoops mashed potato:
3 Points
spinach, carrots and
mushrooms: 0 Points
¹/₂ can Weight Watchers
from Heinz Rice Pudding:
2¹/₂ Points

─────

MILK
600 ml (1 pint) skimmed
milk: 2 Points

TREAT
1 small bag liquorice
allsorts: 2¹/₂ Points

## SUNDAY

BREAKFAST
1 slice bread: 1 Point
1 teaspoon low-fat spread:
¹/₂ Point
1 small banana: 1 Point

♦

LUNCH
*4 Spring Vegetable Filo
Flowers (page 59):*
2 Points
green salad with fat-free
salad dressing: 0 Points
1 tablespoon potato salad:
1 Point
1 tablespoon coleslaw:
1 Point
150 g (5 oz) rhubarb
stewed with sugar: 1 Point

♦

DINNER
*Sausage and Lemon Lentils
(page 53):* 5 Points
1 medium portion boiled
new potatoes: 2 Points
mangetout and grilled
tomatoes: 0 Points
1 small tub low-fat natural
yogurt: 1¹/₂ Points
1 medium slice honeydew
melon: 1 Point

─────

MILK
300 ml (¹/₂ pint) skimmed
milk: 1 Point

TREAT
4 garibaldi biscuits:
2 Points

# March

The first day of spring falls in March, and there is always a degree of optimism as the weather warms up a little. Spinach starts to appear in the shops just as the best of the root vegetables are coming to an end. Because this is an in-between season for fresh produce, it is a good time to take stock if you have a freezer. Use up the remains of last year's produce to make room for the next.

Although the weather is growing milder, there are plenty of days when Oatcakes with Cheese Topping (page 42) would be welcomed at breakfast, or with a bowl of soup. Potatoes feature strongly this month. Wedges with Tomato Sauce (page 49) will make a welcome change from the usual baked potato.

Forced rhubarb is young and pink in March, and makes a delicious Rhubarb Fool (page 54). It is equally tasty simply stewed and sweetened with artificial sweetener for a no-Points pudding.

EGG AND BACON FLORENTINE *(page 52)*
OATCAKES WITH CHEESE TOPPING *(page 42)*
RHUBARB FOOL *(page 54)*

# OATCAKES WITH CHEESE TOPPING

♦

*Makes 8 oatcakes* ♦ *Preparation time 10 minutes* ♦ *Cooking time 10 minutes on a griddle or 20 minutes in the oven* ♦ *Freezing recommended*

*This recipe is an alternative to crispbreads or cream crackers. Although they are served here with cheese, these are equally good for breakfast with a low-sugar jam or marmalade. Oatcakes can be cooked on a griddle (a cast-iron pan), a heavy frying-pan or in the oven. These will keep well if stored in an airtight container.*

Calories per oatcake: 115
Points per oatcake: 2
Total Points per recipe: 16

**FOR THE OATCAKES:**

*120 g (4 oz) oatmeal, plus extra for rolling out*

*2 teaspoons corn or vegetable oil*

*salt*

**FOR THE TOPPING:**

*60 g (2 oz) half-fat cheese, grated*

*60 g (2 oz) fresh dates, stoned and chopped finely*

*1 apple, grated*

*1 teaspoon lemon juice*

*8 sprigs of watercress*

**1** If using the oven, preheat to Gas Mark 3/170°C/325°F.

**2** Put the oatmeal in a bowl and add a pinch of salt.

**3** Add the oil and blend together with a little hot water.

**4** When a stiff paste has formed, turn the mixture on to a clean surface dusted with oatmeal. Knead for 1 minute and then roll out to a 5 mm (¼-inch) thick circle.

**5** If oven-baking, transfer to an oiled baking sheet and cut in eight sections, or 'farls'. Sprinkle with a little oatmeal. Bake for 20 minutes, and then cool on a wire rack.

**6** If cooking on the hob, preheat the grill and the griddle or frying-pan, place the oatcake on the hot surface and cut in eight, Cook for 5 minutes on one side, and then grill the top side until golden brown. Cool on a wire rack.

**7** Meanwhile, make the topping; blend the cheese, chopped dates, grated apple and lemon juice in a bowl. Divide between the oatcakes and top with the watercress.

# SWEETCORN AND MUSHROOM CONSOMMÉ

◆

*Serves 2 ◆ Preparation time 5 minutes ◆ Cooking time 5 minutes ◆ Freezing not recommended*
*Nothing could be simpler than this delicate Chinese-inspired soup. Cans of consommé make an*
*excellent base for healthy soups and can be served either hot or in jellied form,*
*straight from the fridge with a few prawn crackers.*

Calories per serving: 160
Points per serving: 2½
Total Points per recipe: 5

425 g can of beef consommé

1 tablespoon sweetcorn

60 g (2 oz) chestnut mushrooms,
   wiped and sliced thinly

1 teaspoon light soy sauce

1 spring onion, sliced thinly

a small packet of prawn crackers,
   to serve

**1**  Heat the consommé in a pan until almost boiling.

**2**  Add the sweetcorn, mushrooms and soy sauce, and pour immediately into two soup bowls.

**3**  Sprinkle the spring onion on top and serve at once, with the prawn crackers.

# SWEET AND SOUR CABBAGE

◆

*Serves 4 ◆ Preparation time 10 minutes ◆ Cooking time 20 minutes ◆ Freezing not recommended*
*White cabbage, which is normally used for coleslaw, has a very crunchy texture when cooked,*
*but Savoy or green cabbage could be used instead. This recipe takes advantage of the natural*
*sweetness of dried fruits. Serve this by itself or with grilled chicken or fish.*

Calories per serving: 110
Points per serving: 1½
Total Points per recipe: 6

480 g (1 lb) white cabbage, shredded

1 onion, chopped

1 tablespoon vegetable oil

1 garlic clove, sliced

3 tablespoons wine or cider vinegar

30 g (1 oz) sultanas

60 g (2 oz) dried apricots, chopped

salt and freshly ground black pepper

**1**  Put all the ingredients in a pan with a tight-fitting lid.

**2**  Bring to the boil and then lower the heat and simmer for 20 minutes, adding a few spoonfuls of water if necessary.

# CURRIED MEATBALLS WITH CARROT RELISH

◆

*Serves 6 ◆ Preparation time 10 minutes ◆ Cooking time 20 minutes ◆ Freezing recommended*
*Meatballs are served as a starter in Indian restaurants, and are often called kofte.*
*They are usually fried but, if handled carefully, can be grilled instead. The carrot relish makes*
*a change from the tray of pickles offered in restaurants. Serve with some naan bread*
*and a tomato and coriander salad.*

Calories per serving: 210
Points per serving: 3
Total Points per recipe: 18

**FOR THE MEATBALLS:**

*480 g (1 lb) lean minced beef*
   *(see page 63)*

*1 tablespoon wholemeal*
   *breadcrumbs*

*2 garlic cloves, crushed*

*2 teaspoons curry powder*

*1 teaspoon ground cumin*

*1 egg, beaten*

*salt and freshly ground black pepper*

**FOR THE RELISH:**

*4 carrots, peeled and cut in*
   *matchsticks*

*1 tablespoon lemon juice*

*1 tablespoon chopped fresh*
   *coriander*

*¼ teaspoon chilli powder (optional)*

*2 teaspoons vegetable oil*

*salt and freshly ground black pepper*

**1**  Preheat the grill to medium.

**2**  Mix together the meatball ingredients and shape into 16–20 walnut-sized balls.

**3**  Arrange the meatballs on a sheet of foil, and grill for 20 minutes, turning about four times.

**4**  Drain on kitchen paper and keep warm.

**5**  Put the carrots in a small serving dish.

**6**  Whisk together the other relish ingredients and pour over the carrots. Serve alongside the hot meatballs.

CURRIED MEATBALLS WITH CARROT RELISH
ORANGE, ONION AND WATERCRESS SALAD
*(page 46)*

# ORANGE, ONION AND WATERCRESS SALAD

◆

*Serves 1 ◆ Preparation time 10 minutes ◆ Freezing not recommended*
*When the March winds cease and the weather warms up, salads are a pleasant and*
*healthy reminder that spring is on its way. Enjoy this as a light meal or serve with*
*some cold chicken or lean ham.*

Calories per serving: 145
Points per serving: 2

*1 orange, peeled and sliced with*
*    juice reserved (see page 10)*
*1 small red onion, sliced thinly*
*    in rings*
*3 sprigs of watercress*
*5 black olives, halved (optional)*
*1 teaspoon olive oil*
*salt and freshly ground black pepper*

**1**   Arrange the orange and onion slices on a plate.

**2**   Add the watercress and scatter the olives on top.

**3**   Mix together the oil and reserved orange juice and drizzle over the salad. Season and serve.

# DANISH HERRING SALAD

◆

*Serves 4 ◆ Preparation time 10 minutes ◆ Cooking time 20 minutes ◆ Freezing not recommended*
*This makes an inexpensive alternative to smoked salmon and is equally tasty.*
*You can serve this on its own or on crispbreads as an open sandwich.*

Calories per serving: 240
Points per serving: 2½
Total Points per recipe: 10

*240 g (8 oz) salad potatoes*
*340 g jar of pickled or rollmop*
*    herrings*
*2 crisp eating apples, cored and*
*    sliced*
*2 spring onions, sliced*
*150 g tub of low-fat natural yogurt*
*salt and freshly ground black pepper*
*fresh dill, to garnish (optional)*

**1**   Boil the potatoes in their skins and allow to cool. Slice them into a bowl.

**2**   Drain the liquid from the herrings and reserve. Cut the fillets into 2.5 cm (1-inch) squares. Add to the bowl.

**3**   Toss the apple slices in a little of the vinegar from the herring jar to prevent them turning brown. Add them to the bowl with the spring onions.

**4**   Season the yogurt and pour over the top. Garnish with dill fronds, if using.

# PIZZA NAPOLETANA

◆

*Serves 1 ◆ Preparation time 5 minutes ◆ Cooking time 10 minutes◆ Freezing recommended*
*Naples, where this pizza originated, is in the south of Italy, where vegetables and herbs*
*are eaten in preference to meat. I am sure that no self-respecting Neapolitan would use*
*a ready-made pizza base, but it is the quickest way to get a pizza on the table!*

Calories per serving: 335
Points per serving: 3½
Ⓥ if using vegetarian cheese

*200 g can of chopped tomatoes*

*2 teaspoons tomato purée*

*1 garlic clove, crushed*

*1 teaspoon dried mixed herbs*

*75 g ready-made pizza base*

*30 g (1 oz) half-fat mozzarella*
   *cheese, sliced*

*salt and freshly ground black pepper*

**1**  Preheat the oven to Gas Mark 7/220°C/425°F.

**2**  Heat the tomatoes, tomato purée, garlic and herbs in a pan, until reduced and thickened. Season to taste.

**3**  Put the pizza base on a baking sheet and spread the tomato mixture over. Arrange the cheese on top and bake for 10 minutes.

# BUTTER BEAN CRUMBLE

◆

*Serves 2 ◆ Preparation time 5 minutes ◆ Cooking time 30 minutes ◆ Freezing recommended*
*This tasty and satisfying bean casserole could be served as a main meal, with some steamed*
*green vegetables. Otherwise it makes a fine accompaniment for grilled gammon.*

Calories per serving: 300
Points per serving: 4
Total Points per recipe: 8
Ⓥ if using vegetarian cheese

*1 onion, sliced*

*2 garlic cloves, sliced*

*400 g can of chopped tomatoes with*
*herbs*

*430 g can of butter beans, rinsed*
*and drained*

*60 g (2 oz) half-fat cheese, grated*

*60 g (2 oz) wholemeal breadcrumbs*
*(see page 135)*

*½ teaspoon mustard powder*

*salt and freshly ground black pepper*

**1**  Preheat the oven to Gas Mark 5/190°C/375°F.

**2**  Put the onion and garlic in the bottom of a casserole dish. Season well.

**3**  Mix together the tomatoes and beans and pour over the onion.
Season again.

**4**  Mix together the cheese, breadcrumbs and mustard with a little
pepper. Spoon evenly over the casserole.

**5**  Bake for 30 minutes, until golden brown and crisp on top.

**VARIATIONS:** Use flageolet or haricot beans if serving with grilled lamb.
Use red kidney or black-eyed beans with grilled steak. Borlotti beans go
well with grilled fish.

# SWEETCORN AND TUNA BAKED POTATOES

♦

*Serves 1 ♦ Preparation time 10 minutes ♦ Cooking time 1½ hours ♦ Freezing recommended*
*Stuffed baked potatoes make a warming and satisfying light meal. Use your imagination*
*to come up with your own filling ideas.*

Calories per serving: 380
Points per serving: 6½

*1 baking potato*
*100 g can of tuna in oil, drained*
*2 tablespoons sweetcorn*
*1 tablespoon chopped fresh chives*
*salt and freshly ground black pepper*

**1**  Preheat the oven to Gas Mark 6/200°C/400°F.

**2**  Bake the potato for 1 hour or microwave for about 5 minutes (follow the manufacturer's guidelines).

**3**  Halve the potato and scoop out the baked flesh into a bowl.

**4**  Add the drained tuna, sweetcorn and chives, and mash well, adding a little oil from the tuna if necessary. Season well.

**5**  Divide the filling between the two potato shells and return to the oven for 10 minutes, or microwave for 1 minute.

# POTATO WEDGES WITH TOMATO SAUCE

♦

*Serves 2 ♦ Preparation time 5 minutes ♦ Cooking time 45 minutes ♦ Freezing recommended*
*Here's another variation on baked potatoes. The sauce is quick and easy to prepare but, if you*
*want something even quicker, use a jar of ready-made low-Calorie pasta sauce.*

Calories per serving: 140
Points per serving: 2
Total Points per recipe: 4

*1 baking potato, cut in 8 wedges*
*2 teaspoons vegetable oil*
*200 g can of chopped tomatoes*
*1 tablespoon tomato purée*
*1 teaspoon dried mixed herbs*
*salt and freshly ground black pepper*

**1**  Preheat the oven to Gas Mark 7/220°C/425°F.

**2**  Brush the potato wedges with the oil and bake for 30 minutes, turning occasionally.

**3**  Meanwhile, heat the tomatoes in a small saucepan with the tomato purée and herbs, until thickened slightly. Season to taste.

**4**  Transfer the cooked potato wedges to an ovenproof serving dish and spoon the tomato sauce over. Cook for 10 minutes more. Serve hot.

**VARIATION**: If you make this during the summer, use fresh tomatoes and add some chopped fresh basil.

# THAI CHICKEN

◆

*Serves 4* ◆ *Preparation time 10 minutes* ◆ *Cooking time 20 minutes* ◆ *Freezing recommended*
*You should easily find the ingredients needed for a Thai flavour in your supermarket.*
*Although this is a light dish suitable for the beginning of spring, it is spicy and warming.*
*Make your own coconut milk using skimmed milk and desiccated coconut,*
*which contains far less fat than canned coconut milk.*

Calories per serving: 200
Points per serving: 4
Total Points per recipe: 16

*300 ml (½ pint) skimmed milk*

*3 tablespoons unsweetened*
 *desiccated coconut*

*1 tablespoon vegetable oil*

*1 onion, chopped*

*2 garlic cloves, chopped finely*

*2 boneless, skinless chicken breasts,*
 *cut in strips*

*1 green chilli, de-seeded and*
 *chopped finely*

*2.5 cm (1-inch) piece of fresh root*
 *ginger, peeled and chopped finely*

*2 stems of lemon grass, bruised, or*
 *1 teaspoon dried lemon grass*

*1 tablespoon chopped fresh*
 *coriander or 1 tablespoon dried*

*salt*

*fresh coriander leaves, to garnish*
 *(optional)*

**1** Warm the milk and pour it over the coconut. Leave to infuse while you prepare the rest of the ingredients.

**2** Heat the oil in a wok or large frying-pan and stir-fry the onion and garlic for 5 minutes.

**3** Add the chicken strips, chilli, ginger and lemon grass. Stir-fry for 5 minutes more.

**4** Strain the coconut milk and discard the desiccated coconut. Add the coconut milk to the pan, with the chopped coriander, and simmer for 10 minutes.

**5** Season to taste and remove the lemon grass stems, if used. Garnish with coriander leaves, if using, and serve.

**COOK'S NOTE:** To bruise lemon grass, place the leaves on a cutting board and hit them with a rolling pin. This releases the full flavour of the herb. Alternatively, you could use a pinch of dried lemon grass, although the flavour will not be as intense.

SWEETCORN AND MUSHROOM CONSOMMÉ *(page 43)*
THAI CHICKEN
SWEET AND SOUR CABBAGE *(page 43)*

# EGG AND BACON FLORENTINE

◆

*Serves 2 ◆ Preparation time 5 minutes ◆ Cooking time 20 minutes ◆ Freezing not recommended*
*Any dish with the name 'florentine' means that it contains spinach. Fresh, frozen or canned*
*spinach can be used in this recipe. Serve with some crusty bread to mop up the egg bits.*

Calories per serving: 270
Points per serving: 5
Total Points per recipe: 10

*240 g (8 oz) fresh spinach*

*grated nutmeg*

*2 eggs*

*2 tablespoons very-low-fat fromage*
*    frais*

*60 g (2 oz) lean bacon, grilled until*
*    crispy, chopped*

*60 g (2 oz) half-fat Cheddar*
*    cheese, grated*

*salt and freshly ground black pepper*

**1** Wash the spinach and cook for 5 minutes. There is no need to add water, as the spinach will steam in the moisture clinging to its leaves.

**2** Drain and chop, and stir in the grated nutmeg and seasoning. Keep warm.

**3** Poach the eggs in a saucepan or a poaching pan. Preheat the grill.

**4** Mix together the fromage frais, bacon and cheese.

**5** Put the spinach in the bottom of an ovenproof serving dish or two individual dishes.

**6** Create a hollow for each poached egg, and gently set the eggs in them.

**7** Add the fromage frais topping and grill until golden and crisp.

# SAUSAGE AND LEMON LENTILS

◆

*Serves 4 ◆ Preparation time 10 minutes ◆ Cooking time 30 minutes ◆ Freezing recommended*
*Red lentils have a warm colour and comforting texture. They are also very healthy, being*
*a starchy food, high in fibre. They need no pre-soaking and can be prepared and cooked quickly.*
*The lemon in this dish adds a welcome sharpness and the*
*Spanish sausage gives it an extra bite.*

Calories per serving: 400
Points per serving: 5
Total Points per recipe: 20

*1 tablespoon vegetable oil*

*1 onion, chopped*

*1 garlic clove, crushed*

*240 g (8 oz) red lentils*

*600 ml (1 pint) chicken stock*

*grated zest and juice of 1 lemon*

*150 g (5 oz) chorizo sausage or*
  *chipolatas, cut in 2.5 cm (1-inch)*
  *chunks*

*1 tablespoon chopped fresh*
  *coriander*

*salt and freshly ground black pepper*

**1**  Heat the oil in a pan and cook the onion and garlic until soft.

**2**  Stir in the lentils and then add the stock, lemon zest and juice and the sausage chunks.

**3**  Bring to the boil and then reduce the heat and simmer for 30 minutes, or until the lentils are soft and have absorbed the stock.

**4**  Stir in the coriander and season to taste. Serve immediately.

**VARIATION:** Leave out the sausage and use a vegetable stock. Serve with other vegetables, such as carrots and lightly cooked cabbage. This will make it suitable for vegetarians. Points per serving will be 3½.

# RHUBARB FOOL

♦

*Serves 2 ♦ Preparation time 10 minutes ♦ Cooking time 10 minutes + cooling*
*Freezing not recommended*
*The first tender shoots of forced rhubarb are a glorious pink, and go well with fromage frais,*
*which tastes creamy but has few Calories. Serve this with a few ginger biscuits,*
*remembering that each gingernut biscuit costs 1 Point.*

Calories per serving: 80
Points per serving: 2
Total Points per recipe: 4

*360 g (12 oz) rhubarb, chopped in*
*2.5 cm (1-inch) pieces*
*grated zest and juice of 1 small*
*orange*
*about 1 tablespoon granular*
*sweetener*
*200 g tub of very-low-fat fromage*
*frais*

**1**  Cook the rhubarb in a saucepan with the grated orange zest and juice. This will take about 8 minutes.

**2**  Remove from the heat when the rhubarb is soft and add the sweetener to taste. Leave to cool.

**3**  Drain any juice and blend the fruit with the fromage frais, adding just enough juice to give a creamy consistency.

**4**  Pour into two serving bowls and chill.

# QUICK CHOCOLATE MOUSSE

◆

*Serves 3* ◆ *Preparation time 10 minutes + 20 minutes chilling* ◆ *Freezing not recommended*
*There are days when you really feel you have earned a treat. This dessert is for one of those days.*
*Do use good chocolate, definitely not 'cake covering' nor 'couverture'.*

Calories per serving: 215
Points per serving: 5½
Total Points per recipe: 16½

90 g (3 oz) plain chocolate
1 large or 2 small eggs, separated
15 g (½ oz) butter
1 teaspoon brandy (optional)

**1** Break the chocolate into a basin and melt over a pan of simmering water.

**2** Remove from the heat and beat in the egg yolks, butter and brandy, if using.

**3** Whisk the egg whites until stiff, and fold them into the chocolate.

**4** Divide between three small dishes – individual soufflé dishes or ramekins are ideal.

**5** Refrigerate for 20 minutes, until set.

**VARIATION:** A small grating of chocolate would look attractive on top (add 3 Points in total for 25 g chocolate). Double this recipe, using 3 medium-sized eggs, for entertaining. This will reduce the Points to 5 per serving.

# April

Easter usually falls in this month and this is when the first of the new season's lamb, tender and pink, comes into the shops. Tasty and succulent, lamb makes a wonderful meal for family and friends. Do remember to trim any visible fat from the meat before you eat it. A popular and healthy alternative for Easter dinner is turkey. Weight for weight, turkey has less fat than chicken and, now that turkey portions are available all year round, it can be substituted whenever chicken is asked for in a recipe.

As dieting often seems irrelevant to children, make them feel special this month with decorated eggs and other treats. They will love the Spring Vegetable Filo Flowers (page 59) and the Easter Egg Nests (page 61).

The new spring vegetables may be a little costly but are so full of colour and flavour that they're worth the expense. Towards the end of this month, the weather may get warm enough to eat or cook outside. The Tandoori Fish Kebabs (page 64) are ideal for barbecuing or grilling.

EASTER LAMB  *(page 68)*
CARROT AND CHEESE CASTLES *(page 61)*
SPRING VEGETABLE FILO FLOWERS *(page 59)*
LEMON CHEESECAKE *(page 71)*

# SMOKED HADDOCK AND MUSHROOMS

◆

*Serves 2 ◆ Preparation time 10 minutes ◆ Cooking time 10 minutes ◆ Freezing not recommended*
*Smoked haddock has long been a favourite breakfast food and is the key ingredient in a*
*traditional kedgeree. Enjoy this tasty dish on its own, or have it on wholemeal toast. Alternatively,*
*serve it with rice and watercress for a light meal any time of day.*

Calories per serving: 140
Points per serving: 2
Total Points per recipe: 4

*240 g (8 oz) smoked haddock fillet*

*150 ml (¼ pint) skimmed milk*

*2 teaspoons cornflour*

*120 g (4 oz) button mushrooms,*
  *sliced*

*1 teaspoon French mustard*

*1 teaspoon chopped fresh parsley*

*salt and freshly ground black pepper*

**1**  Put the haddock on a heatproof plate. Drizzle with 3 tablespoons of the milk, cover the plate and steam over a pan of boiling water for 10 minutes. Alternatively, microwave the fish for 5 minutes.

**2**  Remove and discard the skin and flake the fish. Transfer the cooking liquid to a pan.

**3**  Blend the cornflour with the cooking liquid and stir in the remainder of the milk.

**4**  Add the mushrooms and bring to the boil, stirring constantly, until thickened. Stir in the mustard.

**5**  Add the flaked fish and heat through.

**6**  Season to taste and stir in the parsley just before serving.

**COOK'S NOTE:** Substitute smoked cod for the haddock.

# SPRING VEGETABLE FILO FLOWERS

♦

*Makes 24 'flowers'* ♦ *Preparation time 15 minutes* ♦ *Cooking time 20 minutes* ♦
*Freezing recommended for pastry flowers only*
*These pastry flowers are as pretty as spring blossoms. You can vary the savoury filling to suit your*
*tastes. Try mixing cooked chicken or canned tuna with the vegetables.*

Calories per 'flower': 60
Points per 'flower': ½
Total Points per recipe: 12

270 g packet of filo pastry, thawed if
   frozen
1 tablespoon vegetable oil
FOR THE FILLING:
240 g (8 oz) baby carrots, topped
   and scrubbed
120 g (4 oz) french beans, topped
   and tailed
a bunch of spring onions, trimmed
   and sliced
200 g can of sweetcorn kernels,
   drained
250 g tub of Quark
1 tablespoon chopped fresh parsley
salt and freshly ground black pepper

**1**   Preheat the oven to Gas Mark 5/190°C/375°F.

**2**   Cut the filo sheets into 8 cm (3-inch) squares. You'll need four squares for each 'flower'.

**3**   Brush a 24-hole bun or tartlet tin with oil.

**4**   Layer four filo squares to form a sixteen-point star, and transfer it carefully to the tin. Repeat with the remaining filo squares, to line all the tin holes.

**5**   Bake for 15 minutes and then cool on a wire rack.

**6**   Meanwhile, plunge the carrots and beans into boiling water and cook for 5 minutes. Rinse in cold water and drain well.

**7**   Mix together the spring onions, sweetcorn, Quark and parsley.

**8**   Finely slice the carrots and beans and fold into the filling mixture.

**9**   Season to taste and spoon the filling into the cooled pastry flowers.

COOK'S NOTES: Keep the filo pastry covered with a damp cloth to prevent it from drying out and becoming brittle.

   The filo flower cases can also be filled with soft fruit and fromage frais for an attractive and tasty dessert.

# LEEK AND POTATO SOUP

♦

*Serves 4 ♦ Preparation time 10 minutes ♦ Cooking time 30 minutes ♦ Freezing recommended*
*This soup can be eaten hot or cold, so is admirably suited for fickle April weather.*

Calories per serving: 90
Points per serving: 1
Total Points per recipe: 4

Ⓥ

1 tablespoon oil

1 onion, chopped

240 g (8 oz) leeks, cleaned and
    sliced

1 potato, peeled and quartered

900 ml (1½ pints) vegetable stock

1 tablespoon chopped fresh chives

salt and freshly ground black pepper

**1**   Heat the oil in a saucepan and cook the onion slowly until soft but not brown.

**2**   Add the leeks and potato to the pan.

**3**   Stir in the stock, bring to the boiling point and then reduce to a simmer and cook for 25 minutes, until the potato is soft.

**4**   Blend the soup in a liquidiser or food processor, or rub through a sieve.

**5**   Reheat and season to taste. Serve hot or cold, sprinkled with chopped chives.

**COOK'S NOTES:** Potatoes are good for thickening soups, but make sure to choose floury maincrop varieties.

You can enrich this soup by adding a little milk or low-fat fromage frais. Don't forget to add the Points.

# CARROT AND CHEESE CASTLES

◆

*Serves 6 ◆ Preparation time 10 minutes + 20 minutes chilling ◆ Freezing not recommended*
*This dish is for one of those April days when you feel the promise of summer. It is light*
*and looks attractive served with a few green salad leaves.*

Calories per serving: 135
Points per serving: 2½
Total Points per recipe: 15
Ⓥ if using vegetarian cheese

*360 g (12 oz) carrots, grated*

*240 g (8 oz) half-fat cheese, grated*

*180 g (6 oz) button mushrooms,*
*    sliced thinly*

*4 tablespoons low-fat vinaigrette*

*1 tablespoon chopped fresh coriander*

*a few mixed green salad leaves*

*3 stoned black olives, halved, to*
*    garnish*

*salt and freshly ground black pepper*

**1** Mix together all the ingredients except the salad leaves and olives. Season to taste.

**2** Pack the mixture into six dariole moulds or small coffee cups. Refrigerate for 20 minutes.

**3** Arrange the salad leaves on six small plates. Turn the carrot and cheese castles out on to the plates. Top each with half an olive.

# EASTER EGG NESTS

◆

*Serves 2 ◆ Preparation time 5 minutes ◆ Cooking time 10 minutes ◆ Freezing not recommended*
*Very often, a simple dish can be transformed by an imaginative presentation. This dish is ideal*
*for Easter but is equally suitable for other times of the year.*

Calories per serving: 180
Points per serving: 3
Total Points per recipe: 6

*1 burger bun or round bread roll,*
*    split in half*

*2 slices of lean ham*

*1 punnet of mustard and cress,*
*    trimmed*

*1 teaspoon vinegar*

*2 eggs*

*salt and freshly ground black pepper*

**1** Toast the bun on both sides and place one half each on two plates.

**2** Put one slice of ham on each half bun, and arrange the cress round the edge, to form 'nests'.

**3** Half-fill a frying-pan with water and bring it to the boil. Add the vinegar.

**4** Break the eggs in, one at a time, and poach for 2–3 minutes.

**5** Remove the eggs with a draining spoon and place one in the middle of each nest. Season well.

**COOK'S NOTE:** This 'nest' idea could be adapted using tiny poached quail's eggs in a nest of alfalfa sprouts or Chinese crispy 'seaweed'.

# SPANISH OMELETTE

◆

*Serves 6 ◆ Preparation time 10 minutes ◆ Cooking time 20 minutes ◆*
*Freezing not recommended*
*The thick Spanish omelette is great for a picnic or packed lunch as it is equally delicious cold*
*as hot. Do use olive oil if you can, as this will improve the flavour.*

Calories per serving: 155
Points per serving: 2½
Total Points per recipe: 15

*1 tablespoon olive oil*

*2 cooked potatoes, cut in 2.5 cm*
*(1-inch) cubes*

*2 Spanish or large onions, chopped*

*6 eggs*

*salt and freshly ground black pepper*

**1**  Heat the oil in a frying-pan and cook the potatoes and onions gently for about 15 minutes, turning occasionally, until golden brown.

**2**  Beat the eggs, season well, and pour over the vegetables. Preheat the grill to medium.

**3**  Cook slowly until the eggs are almost set.

**4**  Put the pan under the grill to brown the top.

**5**  Slide the omelette on to a plate and cut in wedges to serve.

COOK'S NOTE: Other vegetables, such as mushrooms and peppers, can be added. Use fewer onions, so that the volume of the vegetables remains the same.

# MEATLOAF

◆

*Serves 6 ◆ Preparation time 10 minutes ◆ Cooking time 1½ hours ◆ Freezing recommended*
*This is a good way of stretching meat to go a long way. Use the best quality of mince*
*that you can afford as it will contain a higher proportion of lean to fat and the loaf will*
*not shrink as much. Meatloaf can be eaten hot with the Sharp Sauce (recipe below)*
*or cold and sliced, with a salad.*

Calories per serving: 300
Points per serving: 5
Total Points per recipe: 30

*1 onion, grated*
*720 g (1½ lb) extra-lean minced*
  *beef or beef and pork (see below)*
*90 g (3 oz) fresh wholemeal*
  *breadcrumbs (see page 135)*
*1 egg, beaten*
*4 spring onions, sliced thinly*
*1 tablespoon Worcestershire sauce*
*4 rashers streaky bacon*
*salt and freshly ground black pepper*
**FOR THE SHARP SAUCE:**
*juices from the cooked meatloaf*
*1 onion, grated*
*200 g can of chopped tomatoes*
*1 tablespoon vinegar*
*salt and freshly ground black pepper*

1   Preheat the oven to Gas Mark 4/180°C/350°F.

2   Mix together the meatloaf ingredients, except the bacon, until well combined.

3   Stretch the bacon rashers on a work surface with the blunt edge of a knife, and use them to line a 480 g (1 lb) loaf tin.

4   Cover the meatloaf with foil and bake for 1½ hours.

5   Drain off any juices from the cooked meatloaf into a small pan.

6   Add the onion, tomatoes and vinegar to the juices and heat until slightly thickened. Season to taste.

7   Turn out the meatloaf before slicing and serving with the Sharp Sauce.

*Slim Tips*
Supermarkets now label their mince
with the fat content so you can buy the
leanest meat available, whether beef,
pork, lamb, chicken or turkey. To get
rid of as much fat as possible, cook the
mince on its own in a frying-pan and
drain off any fat. Alternatively, grill the
mince in loose patties, allowing fat to
drain from the grill rack on to a piece
of kitchen foil.
◆

# TANDOORI FISH KEBABS

◆

*Serves 4 ◆ Preparation time 5 minutes +1 hour marinating ◆ Cooking time 5–8 minutes ◆*
*Freezing not recommended*

Calories per serving: 135
Points per serving: 1½
Total Points per recipe: 6

3 tablespoons tandoori paste
3 tablespoons low-fat natural yogurt
1 garlic clove, crushed
1 tablespoon lemon juice
1 tablespoon chopped fresh mint
1 green pepper, de-seeded
360 g (12 oz) monkfish or other
   firm-fleshed white fish, cut in
   2.5 cm (1-inch) cubes
2 onions, quartered
salt and freshly ground black pepper

**1**  Mix together the tandoori paste, yogurt, garlic, lemon juice, mint and seasoning. Cut the pepper into 2.5 cm (1-inch) squares.

**2**  Gently turn the fish, onions and pepper in the marinade. Leave for 1 hour, turning occasionally.

**3**  Thread the fish, onions and pepper on to four skewers. Preheat the grill to hot.

**4**  Grill the kebabs for 5–8 minutes, turning occasionally, until the outside begins to char. Serve at once.

**WEIGHT WATCHERS TIP:** Serve these kebabs with a healthy, no-Points tomato, cucumber and coriander salad. Boiled rice or naan bread will round out your meal.

# PASTA BOWS WITH AUBERGINE

◆

*Serves 4 ◆ Preparation time 10 minutes ◆ Cooking time 15 minutes ◆ Freezing recommended*
*The traditional way to cook aubergines is in oil but they are very thirsty vegetables and could*
*play havoc with your Calorie counting. In this recipe they are 'stewed' in tomato juice before*
*being tossed into the pasta. Use any pasta shapes for this dish.*

Calories per serving: 135
Points per serving: 2
Total Points per recipe: 8
Ⓥ

1 aubergine, cubed
2 garlic cloves, crushed
2 tablespoons chopped fresh basil
300 ml (½ pint) tomato juice
120 g (4 oz) pasta shapes
30 g (1 oz) half-fat parmesan
   cheese, grated
salt and freshly ground black pepper

**1**  Combine the aubergine with the garlic, basil, tomato juice and seasoning in a pan, bring to the boil and then simmer for 15 minutes.

**2**  Meanwhile, cook the pasta in plenty of lightly salted boiling water, according to the packet instructions. Drain.

**3**  Return the pasta to the pan and add the aubergine sauce. Toss together and serve topped with grated cheese.

PASTA BOWS WITH AUBERGINE
TANDOORI FISH KEBABS

# CHICKEN LIVER AND MANGETOUT STIR-FRY

◆

*Serves 4 ◆ Preparation time 10 minutes ◆ Cooking time 10 minutes ◆ Freezing not recommended*
*Chicken livers are inexpensive and make a good base for a budget dish. With the addition*
*of brightly coloured vegetables and subtle Chinese seasoning, this is a tasty alternative to*
*a take-away meal. Serve with plain Chinese noodles or boiled rice.*

Calories per serving: 180
Points per serving: 2½
Total Points per recipe: 10

*180 g (6 oz) mangetout, topped and*
*    tailed*

*1 carrot, peeled and sliced thinly*

*360 g (12 oz) chicken livers, thawed*
*    if frozen*

*60 g (2 oz) button mushrooms,*
*    sliced*

*1 tablespoon light soy sauce*

*1 tablespoon dry sherry*

*1 tablespoon vegetable oil*

*1 teaspoon Chinese five-spice*
*    powder*

*2 spring onions, sliced thinly,*
*    to garnish*

**1**  Put the prepared mangetout and carrot in a basin and pour boiling water over. Leave for 2 minutes and drain well.

**2**  Carefully clean the livers and cut off any 'thready' bits. Rinse and pat dry with kitchen paper.

**3**  Slice each liver in three, and place in a basin with the mushrooms. Pour the soy sauce and sherry over the top and leave for 5 minutes.

**4**  Heat the oil and five-spice powder in a wok or frying-pan and stir-fry the liver and mushrooms for 2 minutes or until the livers are sealed. Add the mangetout and carrot and stir-fry for 2 more minutes.

**5**  Transfer to a warm bowl and sprinkle with the spring onions before serving.

# SUN-DRIED TOMATO AND TUNA PASTA BAKE

◆

*Serves 4 ◆ Preparation time 5 minutes ◆ Cooking time 30 minutes ◆ Freezing recommended*
*The concentrated taste of sun-dried tomatoes intensifies the Italian flavours in this*
*quick-and-easy family dish. Serve with a mixed green salad.*

Calories per serving: 385
Points per serving: 4
Total Points per recipe: 16

*1 tablespoon olive oil*

*1 onion, chopped finely*

*2 garlic cloves, crushed*

*1 carrot, peeled and grated*

*2 celery sticks, chopped finely*

*100 g can of tuna in brine, drained*

*400 g can of chopped tomatoes*

*120 g (4 oz) sun-dried tomatoes in*
  *oil, drained and chopped*

*150 ml (¼ pint) white wine*

*240 g (8 oz) pasta shapes (e.g. twists*
  *or penne)*

*1 tablespoon finely grated half-fat*
  *Cheddar cheese*

*1 tablespoon fresh breadcrumbs*

*salt and freshly ground black pepper*

**1** Heat the oven to Gas Mark 5/190°C/375°F.

**2** Heat the oil and gently fry the onion, garlic, carrot and celery until soft.

**3** Stir in the tuna, the tomatoes (canned and sun-dried) and the wine. Cover and simmer gently.

**4** Meanwhile, cook the pasta in lightly salted boiling water for 5 minutes less than the recommended time. Drain well.

**5** Stir the cooked pasta into the sauce, season to taste and pour into an ovenproof dish.

**6** Sprinkle with the grated cheese and breadcrumbs and bake for 15 minutes, or until the top is crunchy.

**COOK'S NOTE:** Use the oil from the sun-dried tomatoes instead of olive oil.

*Slim Tips*
Starchy foods, such as pasta, are good choices for healthy eating; these are high-energy foods, slow to release their energy, giving lasting satisfaction. However, it pays to be careful about what you serve with pasta. Stick to low-fat accompaniments, such as vegetables, fish and lean meats, and choose fewer creamy or cheese-based sauces which are high in Points.
◆

# EASTER LAMB

◆

*Serves 8 ◆ Preparation time 15 minutes ◆ Cooking time 1½ hours ◆ Freezing recommended*
*This dish will be enjoyed by the whole family on Easter Sunday, when the new*
*season's lamb is at its most tender. Ask the butcher to bone the lamb for you or buy a*
*ready-boned leg from the supermarket.*

Calories per serving: 760
Points per serving: 6½
Total Points per recipe: 52

*a boned leg of new season's lamb,*
*   about 1.5–2 kg (3½–4½ lb)*
*120 g (4 oz) ready-to-eat dried*
*   apricots, chopped*
*1 onion, grated*
*60 g (2 oz) fresh wholemeal*
*   breadcrumbs (see page 135)*
*1 tablespoon chopped fresh parsley*
*salt and freshly ground black pepper*

**1**  Preheat the oven to Gas Mark 6/200°C/400°F.

**2**  Lay the meat out on a clean surface and trim away any large pieces of fat.

**3**  Mix together the apricots, onion, breadcrumbs and parsley. Season well.

**4**  Spread the apricot mixture over the meat and roll it up. Fasten securely with string or skewers.

**5**  Place the lamb on a rack over a roasting tin and cook for 1½ hours for rare meat, or slightly longer if you prefer it well done.

**6**  Leave to stand for 10 minutes before carving.

*Kitchen Notes*
Children love decorated eggs.
Egg shells are absorbent, so use only
food colouring to paint directly on the
egg or to dye the water in which the
egg is being boiled. To get a mottled
effect, crack the eggshell carefully after
4 minutes of boiling in coloured water
and then continue boiling for
5–6 minutes.
◆

# ROAST TURKEY WITH MADEIRA SAUCE

♦

*Serves 4 ♦ Preparation time 10 minutes ♦ Cooking time according to weight and
packet instructions ♦ Freezing recommended*
*Turkey is popular for special occasions. In this recipe, a lean breast joint is simply roasted and
served with a well-flavoured wine sauce. Serve it with a selection of fresh vegetables.*

Calories per serving: 220
Points per serving: 2¹/₂
Total Points per recipe: 10

*a turkey breast joint, about 1 kg
(2 lb), skinned*

*2 teaspoons dried mixed herbs*

*1 onion, quartered and stuck
with cloves*

*2 tablespoons plain flour*

*300 ml (¹/₂ pint) chicken stock*

*4 tablespoons Madeira or Marsala
wine or sweet sherry*

*salt and freshly ground black pepper*

**1**   Preheat the oven to Gas Mark 8/230°C/450°F.

**2**   Rub the breast with the herbs and some seasoning.

**3**   Place the onion in a roasting tin and position the joint on top.
Cover with kitchen foil and roast for 1¹/₄–1¹/₂ hours.

**4**   Transfer the joint to a carving board, reserving the pan juices.

**5**   Stir the flour into the juices and add the stock and wine. Boil briskly
for 5 minutes. Season to taste.

**6**   Carve the turkey and serve the sauce separately or pour it over the
sliced meat.

# DRIED FRUIT PUDDING

♦

*Serves 6 ♦ Preparation and cooking time 30 minutes + 1 hour steeping ♦ Freezing not recommended*
*Most people are familiar with the traditional British favourite, Summer Pudding. This variation*
*uses a fruit bread instead of white, and dried fruits instead of soft berries.*

Calories per serving: 230
Points per serving: 4
Total Points per recipe: 24

Ⓥ

*300 ml (½ pint) unsweetened*
   *orange juice*
*1 teaspoon ground mixed spice*
*250 g packet of dried fruit salad,*
   *chopped finely, with stones*
   *removed if necessary*
*60 g (2 oz) raisins*
*225 g (7½ oz) malt loaf*

**1**  Heat the orange juice and spice in a pan and add the dried fruit and raisins. Remove from the heat and leave to steep for 1 hour.

**2**  Bring to the boil and simmer for 20 minutes. Drain well, reserving the juices.

**3**  Meanwhile, slice the loaf and line a 600 ml (1 pint) basin with the slices, overlapping where necessary and reserving two slices.

**4**  Fill the bread-lined basin with the fruit and add juice to moisten. (If there are any juices left over, boil them up with a teaspoon of arrowroot, to make a sauce for your pudding.)

**5**  Cover with the reserved bread and place a weighted plate or saucer on the top. Leave overnight in a cool place.

**6**  Before serving, loosen the edges and turn out on a plate.

# LEMON CHEESECAKE

◆

*Serves 8 ◆ Preparation and cooking time 25 minutes + 3–4 hours chilling ◆*
*Freezing recommended*

*This is a lovely dessert for entertaining family or friends at Easter. The refreshing flavour and*
*creamy texture belie this cheesecake's true low-fat and low-Calorie nature.*

Calories per serving: 215
Points per serving: 4
Total Points per recipe: 32
Ⓥ if using a gelatine substitute

*210 g (7 oz) digestive biscuits,*
  *crushed*
*60 g (2 oz) low-fat spread, melted*

**FOR THE CHEESECAKE:**

*1 sachet of powdered gelatine*
*grated zest and juice of 1 large*
  *lemon*
*2 tablespoons hot water*
*250 g tub of Quark*
*2 tablespoons granular artificial*
  *sweetener*
*2 eggs, separated*
*150 g tub of low-fat natural yogurt*

**TO DECORATE:**

*lemon slices*
*15 g (½ oz) unsalted pistachio nuts,*
  *chopped*

**1** Combine the biscuit crumbs and melted spread and press the mixture into the base of a 20 cm (8-inch) loose-bottomed flan tin. Transfer to the refrigerator.

**2** Sprinkle the gelatine over the lemon juice and hot water in a basin. Leave for a few minutes and then set the basin over a pan of simmering water.

**3** Stir until the gelatine has dissolved and then set to one side.

**4** Mix together the Quark and sweetener in a large bowl. Beat in the egg yolks and lemon zest. Stir in the gelatine and the yogurt.

**5** Whisk the egg whites in a large bowl until stiff and then fold them into the lemon mixture.

**6** Pour the mixture into the flan tin and refrigerate for 2–3 hours.

**7** Before serving, slide a knife round the edge of the tin and remove the outer ring, by placing the base on a jam jar or cup and pushing down.

**8** Leaving the base in place, put the cheesecake on a pretty plate and decorate it with the lemon slices and chopped pistachios.

**WEIGHT WATCHERS TIPS:** If you want to make this dessert a little lighter still, simply omit the base and pour the lemon cheese mixture into a pretty bowl to chill. This would reduce the Points to 1 per serving and the Calories to 70 per serving.

Because this dish contains uncooked eggs, pregnant women, young children, elderly people, and those particularly susceptible to infection should not eat it.

# May

Make the most of late spring vegetables, especially the home-grown broad beans and mangetout or snow peas. They are equally good in salads or stir-fries.

Herrings and mackerel are in season, and are very tasty as well as being good for you. As with other oily fish, these contain significant amounts of omega-3 fatty acids, which are thought to guard against heart disease. Grill or bake these fish so that no extra fat is added. A sharp fruity sauce works well with them – I have suggested gooseberry, but rhubarb or apple would be equally delicious.

Herbs are inexpensive and plentiful now, so use them liberally to enhance flavours and add colour to meals. Nothing perks up a tomato salad better than a handful of fresh chopped basil, for instance.

GRILLED MACKEREL WITH GOOSEBERRIES *(page 79)*
SPRING VEGETABLE PASTA *(page 82)*
BANANA TRIFLE *(page 87)*

# YOGURT WITH BANANAS

◆

*Serves 1 ◆ Preparation time 5 minutes ◆ Freezing not recommended*
*Adding your own flavours to yogurt can be healthier than buying ready-prepared varieties,*
*as they often contain a lot of sugar. This quick recipe makes a great start to any day.*

Calories per serving: 240
Points per serving: 5½

1  Mix the yogurt with the sliced banana and dried fruit.
2  Sprinkle with cinnamon and scatter the sunflower seeds on top.
3  Refrigerate until ready to serve.

*150 g tub of low-fat natural yogurt*

*1 banana, sliced*

*2 teaspoons sultanas or raisins*

*¼ teaspoon ground cinnamon*

*2 teaspoons sunflower seeds*

# DIPS AND STRIPS

◆

*Serves 4 ◆ Preparation time 15 minutes ◆ Freezing not recommended*
*This colourful light meal can be varied according to the ingredients available.*
*Apple or pear slices, baby sweetcorn and mushrooms all make great dippers.*

Calories per serving: 115
Points per serving: 1
Total Points per recipe: 4

1  Peel the carrots, and cut carrots and celery into 7.5 cm (3-inch) matchsticks. Cut the cauliflower into bite-size florets. Halve and de-seed the peppers and cut into strips. Arrange the vegetables on a platter.
2  Mix together the dip ingredients and serve in a bowl placed on the vegetable platter.

COOK'S NOTE: For a change of taste, flavour your dip with fresh salsa, chopped herbs, or a spoonful of curry paste.

*2 carrots*

*4 celery sticks*

*1 small cauliflower*

*1 red pepper*

*1 green pepper*

**FOR THE DIP:**

*300 g tub of low-fat natural yogurt*

*1 teaspoon concentrated mint sauce*

*1 garlic clove, crushed*

*6 radishes, topped, tailed and*
   *chopped finely*

*salt and freshly ground black pepper*

# PEPERONATA

◆

*Serves 4 ◆ Preparation time 10 minutes ◆ Cooking time 30 minutes ◆ Freezing recommended*
*This ratatouille-type dish can be enjoyed on its own or eaten with toast or bread. Poached eggs*
*(page 61) are also good with this spicy vegetable dish.*

Calories per serving: 125
Points per serving: 1½
Total Points per recipe: 6

2 tablespoons olive oil

1 onion, chopped

2 garlic cloves, sliced

4 peppers, assorted colours,
   de-seeded and sliced

400 g can of chopped tomatoes

2 teaspoons sherry or balsamic
   vinegar (optional)

salt and freshly ground black pepper

**1**  Heat the olive oil in a pan and cook the onion and garlic over a low heat, until soft but not browned.

**2**  Add the sliced peppers and cook for 20 minutes more.

**3**  Stir in the tomatoes and cook for 5 more minutes.

**4**  Add the vinegar just before serving, if using, and season well.

# SPINACH SOUP

◆

*Serves 4 ◆ Preparation time 10 minutes ◆ Cooking time 30 minutes ◆ Freezing recommended*
*This bright green soup is packed with minerals and vitamins and can be served hot or cold.*
*It can be made with fresh or frozen spinach.*

Calories per serving: 120
Points per serving: 1
Total Points per recipe: 4

*1 tablespoon vegetable oil*

*1 onion, chopped*

*2 garlic cloves, chopped*

*240 g (8 oz) fresh spinach, rinsed*
  *and drained*

*1.2 litres (2 pints) vegetable stock*

*2 potatoes, peeled and cut in small*
  *pieces*

*1 teaspoon grated nutmeg*

*salt and freshly ground black pepper*

**1**  Heat the oil in a large pan and cook the onion and garlic slowly, until soft but not browned.

**2**  Add the spinach, stock, potatoes and nutmeg.

**3**  Bring to the boil and then cover and simmer for 25 minutes.

**4**  Liquidise in batches or whizz in a food processor.

**5**  Season to taste and serve in warm bowls.

**COOK'S NOTES**: Spinach needs careful washing to remove all traces of the sandy grit in which it is grown.

You could use other leafy vegetables, such as kale or Savoy cabbage, in this recipe.

# SOFT ROES AND MUSHROOMS ON MUFFINS

◆

*Serves 2 ◆ Preparation time 10 minutes ◆ Cooking time 10 minutes ◆ Freezing not recommended*
*Nutritious and quick to cook, soft roes make an excellent light meal and their mild flavour*
*blends well with the tastes of the other ingredients.*

Calories per serving: 175
Points per serving: 3
Total Points per recipe: 6

*zest and juice of 1 lemon*

*240 g (8 oz) soft herring roes,*
  *rinsed, with any threads removed*

*120 g (4 oz) button mushrooms,*
  *sliced*

*1 teaspoon Worcestershire sauce*

*1 muffin, split in half*

*paprika and chopped fresh parsley,*
  *to garnish*

**1**  Heat the lemon juice and zest in a small pan and add the roes. Stir until the outside of the roes is firm.

**2**  Stir in the mushrooms and Worcestershire sauce and cook for 3 minutes.

**3**  Meanwhile, toast the muffin halves on both sides.

**4**  Spoon the roes and mushrooms on top of the muffin halves, dust with the paprika and sprinkle with the chopped parsley. Serve at once.

# INDIAN CHICKEN SANDWICH

◆

*Serves 1 ◆ Preparation time 10 minutes ◆ Freezing not recommended*
*Naan bread makes the perfect base for the spicy taste of tandoori or curried chicken.*
*However, you could put this tasty filling between two slices of any bread you like.*

Calories per serving: 250
Points per serving: 6½

1 small naan bread

60 g (2 oz) ready-cooked lean
   tandoori or curried chicken,
   chopped coarsely

1 teaspoon mango chutney

1 teaspoon chopped fresh mint

2 teaspoons low-fat natural yogurt

2 lettuce leaves, shredded

4 slices of cucumber

¼ lemon

salt and freshly ground black pepper

**1** Warm the bread in a microwave or under a low grill.

**2** Mix the chicken with the chutney, mint and yogurt.

**3** Season to taste and spread on the naan bread.

**4** Garnish with lettuce and cucumber and squeeze the lemon over the top before eating.

**WEIGHT WATCHERS TIP:** As naan bread comes in packets, freeze the rest right away. That way you'll be less inclined to nibble on an extra one while you're preparing your sandwich.

# SCALLOPED POTATOES AND MINCE

♦

*Serves 2 ♦ Preparation time 10 minutes ♦ Cooking time 30 minutes ♦ Freezing recommended*
*This is a convenient dish which will keep well in a low oven. If you are entertaining,*
*increase the ingredients accordingly to make a larger dish.*

Calories per serving: 380
Points per serving: 5½
Total Points per recipe: 11

*180 g (6 oz) extra-lean minced beef*
*or lamb (see page 63)*
*1 onion, chopped*
*360 g (12 oz) potatoes, peeled and*
*cut in 5 mm (¼-inch) slices*
*150 ml (¼ pint) beef stock*
*1 tablespoon tomato purée*
*3 tablespoons half-fat cheese, grated*
*salt and freshly ground black pepper*

**1**  Preheat the oven to Gas Mark 6/200°C/400°F.

**2**  Mix the minced beef or lamb with the onion and season well.

**3**  Put one-third of the mince in a small casserole and add a layer of potatoes. Season.

**4**  Repeat the layers twice more, saving the best potato slices for the top.

**5**  Mix together the stock and tomato purée and pour over the casserole.

**6**  Top with grated cheese and bake for 30 minutes, or until the potatoes are tender.

**7**  Cover the top with kitchen foil if the casserole begins to brown too much.

**COOK'S NOTE:** This dish can be microwaved on HIGH (100%) for 10 minutes. Cover it with clingfilm for the first 8 minutes and place under a hot grill to crisp the top.

# GRILLED MACKEREL WITH GOOSEBERRIES

◆

*Serves 2 ◆ Preparation time 10 minutes ◆ Cooking time 10 minutes ◆*
*Freezing recommended for the sauce and for the uncooked mackerel (if not previously frozen)*
*It is a happy coincidence that mackerel and gooseberries are both at their best this month,*
*as they go so well together, the acidity of the fruit cutting through the oily fish.*
*Ask the fishmonger to remove the head and fillet the fish if you don't want to do it yourself*

Calories per serving: 300
Points per serving: 5
Total Points per recipe: 10

*2 small or 1 large mackerel, filleted*

*1 tablespoon oatmeal*

*1 teaspoon mustard powder*

*240 g (8 oz) gooseberries, topped*
  *and tailed*

*2 tablespoons water*

*artificial sweetener, to taste*

*salt and freshly ground black pepper*

**1**  Wash the mackerel and pat dry with kitchen paper.

**2**  Mix together the oatmeal and mustard powder with a little seasoning. Press into the flesh side of the mackerel.

**3**  Put the gooseberries and water in a pan, bring to the boil and simmer until mushy. (This could also be done in a microwave.) Rub through a sieve.

**4**  Taste the gooseberry sauce before adding the minimum amount of sweetener – the taste should be sharp.

**5**  Place the mackerel on a sheet of foil, and grill first the skin side for 3 minutes, and then the oatmeal-coated side for 5 minutes. Serve the sauce separately.

**COOK'S NOTE:** You can cook the gooseberries at the same time as you grill the mackerel. They do not take long to rub through the sieve.

# COD IN A PARCEL

◆

*Serves 4 ◆ Preparation time 10 minutes ◆ Cooking time 15 minutes ◆ Freezing not recommended*
*Opening parcels is always exciting and, when these foil packages are opened, a delicious aroma*
*will waft out. The fresh cod will be moist and cooked to perfection.*

Calories per serving: 130
Points per serving: 2
Total Points per recipe: 8

*4 × 120 g (4 oz) pieces of middle-*
*cut cod fillet, skinned*

*1 carrot, peeled and grated*

*1 courgette, topped, tailed and*
*grated*

*1 tomato, skinned (see page 109),*
*de-seeded and chopped*

*1 onion, chopped*

*1 tablespoon horseradish sauce*

*1 tablespoon chopped fresh parsley*

*4 teaspoons lemon juice*

*salt and freshly ground black pepper*

**1**  Preheat the oven to Gas Mark 8/230°C/450°F.

**2**  Cut four 30 cm (12-inch) squares of kitchen foil.

**3**  Place a piece of cod on each square and season well.

**4**  Mix together the carrot, courgette, tomato, onion, horseradish
and parsley.

**5**  Divide the vegetables between the parcels and arrange on top and
around the cod. Drizzle with the lemon juice and season again.

**6**  Wrap the parcels up and seal tightly. Place on a baking sheet and bake
at the top of the oven for 15 minutes.

**7**  Serve the sealed parcels on warm plates.

**COOK'S NOTE:** If you're feeling adventurous, add a teaspoon of sherry,
white wine, vermouth or pastis to the lemon juice, and ½ Point to the total
recipe. Serve with mashed potatoes and extra carrots and courgettes.

# SPRING VEGETABLE PASTA

♦

*Serves 4 ♦ Preparation time 10 minutes ♦ Cooking time 15 minutes ♦ Freezing recommended*
*The lightly cooked spring vegetables, with their crunchy textures and bright colours,*
*provide a tasty foil for the softer pasta.*

Calories per serving: 320
Points per serving: 4
Total Points per recipe: 16

240 g (8 oz) pasta bows (or other
   pasta shapes)
120 g (4 oz) french beans, topped,
   tailed and cut in 5 cm (2-inch)
   lengths
240 g (8 oz) thin leeks, cleaned and
   sliced on the diagonal
1 tablespoon vegetable oil
1 onion, chopped
120 g (4 oz) young carrots, sliced
   on the diagonal
240 g (8 oz) chestnut mushrooms,
   sliced
120 g (4 oz) frozen petits pois
2 tablespoons chopped fresh parsley
250 g tub of very-low-fat fromage
   frais
salt and freshly ground black pepper

**1** Cook the pasta in lightly salted boiling water according to the packet instructions and drain.

**2** Meanwhile, pour boiling water over the beans and leeks, and blanch for 3 minutes (see page 128).

**3** Heat the oil in a wok or frying-pan and stir-fry the onion, carrots, mushrooms and peas for 5 minutes.

**4** Stir in the parsley, fromage frais and blanched vegetables and season to taste.

**5** Transfer the drained pasta to a serving bowl and toss with the vegetables. Serve at once.

# CREAMED BROAD BEANS WITH HAM

◆

*Serves 2 ◆ Preparation time 5 minutes ◆ Cooking time 15 minutes ◆*
*Freezing not recommended*

*Ham is often considered a fatty meat but, as most of the fat is 'visible' and can be trimmed away,*
*it is actually low in fat. Fresh broad beans are just coming into the shops this month, but frozen*
*beans could be used instead. Serve with a plain baked potato or some crusty bread.*

Calories per serving: 210
Points per serving: 3
Total Points per recipe: 6

*240 g (8 oz) broad beans, shelled*
*150 ml (¹/₄ pint) skimmed milk*
*1 tablespoon cornflour*
*1 tablespoon chopped fresh parsley*
*120 g (4 oz) lean cooked ham, cut*
*  in strips or chunks*
*4 spring onions, sliced*
*salt and freshly ground black pepper*

**1**   Cook the broad beans in boiling water for 6 minutes. Drain and reserve 150 ml (¹/₄ pint) of the cooking liquid.
**2**   Blend the milk with the cornflour and bring to the boil with the reserved cooking liquid, stirring constantly, until thickened.
**3**   Stir in the cooked beans, parsley, ham and spring onions. Season to taste.

**COOK'S NOTES:** Vegetarians could omit the ham. Points per serving will be 1¹/₂. Other vegetables which would go well in this creamy sauce are onions (which should be cooked for 30 minutes), cooked beetroot (which will turn the sauce the most wonderful pink colour), or peas and leeks.

# SMOKED SALMON ROLLS

◆

*Serves 2 ◆ Preparation time 10 minutes ◆ Freezing not recommended*

*Ready-made smoked salmon rolls can be very expensive. However, these are simple to make, and*
*you'll find smoked salmon offcuts are much less expensive than buying full slices.*

Calories per serving: 340
Points per serving: 5
Total Points per recipe: 10

*120 g (4 oz) smoked salmon offcuts*
*250 g tub of Quark*
*1 tablespoon chopped fresh chives or*
*  dill*
*4 slices of wholemeal bread, crusts*
*  removed*
*¹/₂ lemon, cut in 4 wedges*
*salt and freshly ground black pepper*

**1**   Choose four of the largest smoked salmon pieces and smooth them out with the back of a knife.
**2**   Chop the remaining pieces quite small and mix them with the Quark, reserving four teaspoons for garnish.
**3**   Beat in the chives or dill, reserving four pinches for garnish.
**4**   Season with a little salt and lots of black pepper.
**5**   Divide the mixture between the four smoked salmon pieces, and roll them up as neatly as possible.
**6**   Toast the bread on both sides and place a salmon roll on each toast. Garnish each with the reserved Quark, chopped herbs and a wedge of lemon.

# CHICKEN AND VEGETABLE TERRINE

◆

*Serves 6 ◆ Preparation time 15 minutes ◆ Cooking time 1 hour ◆ Freezing recommended*
*This pretty striped terrine makes a lovely warm-weather dish when served with salad.*
*A food processor or liquidiser is necessary to get a really smooth texture. It may seem a bit fiddly,*
*but the spectacular results are worth it.*

Calories per serving: 130
Points per serving: 2
Total Points per recipe: 12

*120 g (4 oz) cooked lean chicken*

*360 g (12 oz) Quark*

*3 eggs*

*1 tablespoon chopped fresh chives*

*120 g (4 oz) cooked or canned*
  *spinach*

*½ teaspoon grated nutmeg*

*120 g (4 oz) baby carrots, cooked*

*½ teaspoon ground cumin*

*oil, for brushing*

*salt and freshly ground black pepper*

**1**  Preheat the oven to Gas Mark 3/160°C/325°F.

**2**  Place the chicken, one-third of the Quark and one egg in the food processor and blend until smooth. Add the chives and seasoning and transfer to a bowl.

**3**  Next, process the spinach, another third of Quark, another egg and the nutmeg. Transfer to a bowl. Finally blend together the carrots with the remaining Quark, egg and cumin.

**4**  Brush a 480 g (1 lb) loaf tin with oil, and spoon in the chicken mixture. Level off, using a palette knife.

**5**  Spoon on the carrot, level off, and then top with the spinach.

**6**  Place the loaf tin in a roasting tin half-filled with water (bain-marie). This will prevent the terrine from overcooking and drying out.

**7**  Cook for 1 hour. Remove from the oven and bain-marie, allow to cool, and then turn out on to a serving plate.

**COOK'S NOTE:** This could be served with a tomato and orange sauce, made by simply mixing passata (sieved tomato) and the juice of an orange with some seasoning and chopped fresh chives. This will be just ½ Point in total.

CHICKEN AND VEGETABLE TERRINE
SMOKED SALMON ROLLS *(page 83)*

# POACHED APRICOTS WITH NUTMEG SAUCE

◆

*Serves 2 ◆ Preparation time 5 minutes ◆ Cooking time 10 minutes ◆ Freezing not recommended*
*I can never resist fresh apricots when they first appear in the shops –*
*they have such a wonderful colour, soft skin and sweet aroma. It's amazing that*
*I ever get round to cooking them.*

Calories per serving: 110
Points per serving: 2
Total Points per recipe: 4

*240 g (8 oz) fresh apricots, halved*
*   and stones removed*
*6 tablespoons unsweetened orange*
*   juice*
*artificial sweetener, to taste*
*1 small tub low-fat apricot yogurt*
*½ teaspoon grated nutmeg*

**1**   Put the apricots and orange juice in a pan, cover and simmer for
10 minutes.

**2**   Remove from the heat and add artificial sweetener to taste.
Transfer to two serving bowls.

**3**   Stir the yogurt until smooth and dollop on to the apricots.
Sprinkle with nutmeg and serve.

**COOK'S NOTE:** You can serve the apricots warm, or chill them and enjoy
them cold. However, the yogurt should be served chilled.

# BANANA TRIFLE

◆

*Serves 4 ◆ Preparation time 15 minutes ◆ Freezing not recommended*
*This would make a special dessert for a bank holiday weekend. Trifle sponges are made with a*
*fatless cake mixture and so, with the fromage frais topping, there is very little fat in this trifle.*
*For an extra-special trifle, 2 tablespoons of dry sherry could be added with the orange juice.*

Calories per serving: 355
Points per serving: 3½
Total Points per recipe: 14

*4 trifle sponges*

*about 150 ml (¼ pint) unsweetened*
*orange juice*

*2 bananas, sliced*

*1 tablespoon lemon juice*

*300 ml (½ pint) ready-made cold*
*custard*

*200 ml tub of very-low-fat fromage*
*frais*

*1 orange, segmented (see page 10)*

**1**  Arrange the trifle sponges in the bottom of a glass serving bowl or divide between individual glasses.

**2**  Drizzle the orange juice over to moisten the sponges.

**3**  Toss the banana slices in the lemon juice, to prevent them from browning.

**4**  Arrange three-quarters of the banana slices over the sponge layer.

**5**  Mix together the custard and fromage frais until smooth and spread over the bananas.

**6**  Garnish with the remaining banana slices and the orange segments.

*Kitchen Notes*
Ready-made custard in cartons or cans makes light work of preparing desserts. However, if you prefer to make your own using artificial sweetener, remember to stir it occasionally as it cools, to prevent a skin from forming on top.

◆

*Summer*

•

# MENU PLAN

## MONDAY

**BREAKFAST**
1 small glass fruit juice:
$^1/_2$ Point
mushrooms stir-fried in
1 teaspoon vegetable oil:
1 Point
1 slice toast: 1 Point
1 teaspoon low-fat spread:
$^1/_2$ Point
◆
**LUNCH**
*Pan Bagnat (page 133):*
$5^1/_2$ Points
1 nectarine or peach:
$^1/_2$ Point
◆
**DINNER**
1 medium pork loin chop
grilled: 5 Points
2 scoops mashed potato:
2 Points
courgettes and carrots:
0 Points
2 tablespoons peas:
1 Point
gravy made with 1
teaspoon gravy granules:
$^1/_2$ Point
green salad with fat-free
salad dressing: 0 Points

————

**MILK**
600 ml (1 pint) skimmed
milk: 2 Points
**TREAT**
1 medium portion
cherries: $^1/_2$ Point

## TUESDAY

**BREAKFAST**
1 medium bowl
cornflakes: $1^1/_2$ Points
150 ml ($^1/_4$ pint) skimmed
milk: $^1/_2$ Point
1 small banana: 1 Point
◆
**LUNCH**
omelette made with
2 eggs and 1 teaspoon
vegetable oil: 4 Points
salad of mushrooms,
lettuce, radishes and
spring onions with
fat-free salad dressing:
0 Points
1 slice bread: 1 Point
1 teaspoon low-fat spread:
$^1/_2$ Point
◆
**DINNER**
*Chicken Kebabs
(page 114):* 2 Points
1 medium portion cooked
rice: 3 Points
1 large portion sweetcorn:
$^1/_2$ Point
tomato salad: 0 Points
1 peach or nectarine:
$^1/_2$ Point

————

**MILK**
450 ml ($^3/_4$ pint) skimmed
milk: $1^1/_2$ Points
**TREAT**
4 Jaffa cakes: 4 Points

## WEDNESDAY

**BREAKFAST**
$^1/_2$ grapefruit with granular
artificial sweetener:
$^1/_2$ Point
1 slice toast: 1 Point
1 teaspoon low-fat spread:
$^1/_2$ Point
◆
**LUNCH**
1 medium portion prawns:
1 Point
1 tablespoon coleslaw:
1 Point
2 tablespoons potato salad:
2 Points
salad of cucumber, lettuce,
mangetout and red pepper
with fat-free salad
dressing: 0 Points
6 fresh apricots: 1 Point
◆
**DINNER**
*Grilled Salmon with Fresh
Tomato Salsa
(page 118):* 3 Points
1 large portion cooked
rice: $4^1/_2$ Points
*Pineapple Boats
(page 105):* 1 Point

**MILK**
600 ml (1 pint)
skimmed milk: 2 Points
**TREAT**
$^1/_2$ can Weight Watchers
from Heinz Rice
Pudding: $2^1/_2$ Points

| THURSDAY | FRIDAY | SATURDAY | SUNDAY |
|---|---|---|---|
| BREAKFAST | BREAKFAST | BREAKFAST | BREAKFAST |
| 1 small glass fruit juice: $^1/_2$ Point | 2 slices toast: 2 Points | $^1/_2$ grapefruit with granular artificial sweetener: $^1/_2$ Point | 1 small glass fruit juice: $^1/_2$ Point |
| 1 large boiled egg: 2 Points | 2 teaspoons low-fat spread: 1 Point | 1 oatcake: 1 Point | 1 medium bowl cornflakes: $1^1/_2$ Points |
| 1 slice bread: 1 Point | 2 heaped teaspoons jam or marmalade: 1 Point | 1 teaspoon low-fat spread: $^1/_2$ Point | 150 ml ($^1/_4$ pint) skimmed milk: $^1/_2$ Point |
| 1 teaspoon low-fat spread: $^1/_2$ Point | 1 small tub low-fat natural yogurt: $1^1/_2$ Points | ◆ | ◆ |
| ◆ | ◆ | LUNCH | LUNCH |
| LUNCH | LUNCH | 1 medium baked potato: $2^1/_2$ Points | *Spaghetti with Summer Vegetables (page 131):* 5 Points |
| *Pasta Salad Niçoise (page 113):* 3 Points | 3 Ryvita: $1^1/_2$ Points | 2 teaspoons low-fat spread: 1 Point | green salad with fat-free salad dressing: 0 Points |
| a 5 cm (2-inch) slice french bread: $1^1/_2$ Points | 1 small carton (120 g/4 oz) low-fat soft cheese: 3 Points | 1 slice low-fat cheese: 1 Point | 1 peach or nectarine: $^1/_2$ Point |
| 1 small tub low-fat natural yogurt: $1^1/_2$ Points | salad of tomato, cucumber and onion with fat-free salad dressing: 0 Points | green salad with fat-free salad dressing: 0 Points | 1 slice bread: 1 Point |
| ◆ | 2 rings pineapple in natural juice: $^1/_2$ Point | 1 small tub low-fat natural yogurt: $1^1/_2$ Points | 1 teaspoon low-fat spread: $^1/_2$ Point |
| DINNER | ◆ | 1 medium portion blackcurrants or raspberries: $^1/_2$ Point | ◆ |
| 1 medium fillet grilled plaice: 2 Points | DINNER | ◆ | DINNER |
| 2 scoops mashed potato: 2 Points | *Liver and Broccoli Stir-fry in Tortillas (page 152):* 8 Points | DINNER | 1 medium fillet smoked haddock: 1 Point |
| broccoli, mangetout and carrots: 0 Points | | *Spiced Beef Patties (page 132):* 3 Points | 1 large poached egg: 2 Points |
| 1 small can (210 g/7 oz) fruit cocktail in natural juice: 1 Point | | grilled tomatoes and steamed courgettes: 0 Points | 3 scoops mashed potato: 3 Points |
| | | *Cherry and Muesli Sundae (page 121):* $3^1/_2$ Points | broccoli and carrots: 0 Points |
| | | | *Kissel (page 120):* $1^1/_2$ Points |
| MILK | MILK | MILK | MILK |
| 300 ml ($^1/_2$ pint) skimmed milk: 1 Point | 300 ml ($^1/_2$ pint) skimmed milk: 1 Point | 300 ml ($^1/_2$ pint) skimmed milk: 1 Point | 450 ml ($^3/_4$ pint) skimmed milk: $1^1/_2$ Points |
| TREAT | TREAT | TREAT | TREAT |
| 1 Cornetto ice-cream cone: 4 Points | 1 medium slice cantaloupe melon: $^1/_2$ Point | 1 small bag tortilla chips: 4 Points | Weight Watchers from Heinz low-fat Chocolate Mousse: $1^1/_2$ Points |

# June

June is the month when those great foods which are part of the typical British summer scene are at their best – salmon, strawberries and asparagus. These are all foods which are low in Points, so make the most of them during their short, home-grown season.

New potatoes are delicious in salads and served hot, sprinkled with chopped fresh herbs. They don't need peeling: just give them a scrubbing and then steam or boil them. The soft summer fruits with their high vitamin and fibre content are superb on their own, but you can use those which are slightly past their best by crushing them into a purée and whipping them into mousses or fools.

SALMON WITH YOGURT HOLLANDAISE *(page 99)*
ASPARAGUS WITH BACON BOWS *(page 95)*
WARM BEEF AND POTATO SALAD *(page 98)*
STRAWBERRY AND RASPBERRY MOUSSE *(page 104)*

# BAKED EGG IN A TOMATO SHELL

*Serves 1 ♦ Preparation time 5 minutes ♦ Cooking time 10 minutes ♦ Freezing not recommended*
*Although I've included this recipe as a breakfast dish, it could equally well be enjoyed as a light*
*meal, perhaps with a different seasoning. Choose well flavoured tomatoes.*

Calories per serving: 200
Points per serving: 3½

1 large tomato
½ teaspoon vegetable oil
1 egg
1 slice of bread
salt and freshly ground black pepper

**1**  Preheat the oven to Gas Mark 4/180°C/350°F.

**2**  Cut a small lid from the top of the tomato.

**3**  Carefully scoop out the seeds and discard.

**4**  Stand the tomato shell on a small baking tin and season the inside. If it wobbles, slice a thin piece off its bottom.

**5**  Spoon in the oil, break the egg into the tomato and season again. Replace the lid, and bake for 10 minutes. Toast the bread just before the egg is ready.

**6**  Slide the tomato on to the toast and serve at once.

**COOK'S NOTE:** Baked eggs in tomato shells can be made more substantial by adding some mozzarella cheese and chopped bacon to the tomato. Remember to add the extra Points.

# BRUSCHETTA AND ANTIPASTI

◆

*Serves 2 ◆ Preparation time 10 minutes ◆ Cooking time 5 minutes ◆ Freezing not recommended*
*The Mediterranean region is known for its healthy eating patterns. This easy light meal,*
*an Italian open sandwich, demonstrates why this style of eating works so well. Ciabatta*
*is an Italian bread made with olive oil. It is now found in most supermarkets.*
*Buy a loaf if you are planning to use more at another meal; otherwise, buy a roll.*
*Tapenade is an olive paste and bresaola is an Italian cured beef. Both should be available*
*in the delicatessen section of your supermarket.*

Calories per serving: 205
Points per serving: 3½
Total Points per recipe: 7

*1 ciabatta roll, split in 2, or 2 thick*
*    slices of ciabatta bread*
*1 garlic clove, peeled and cut*
*    in half*
*1 teaspoon olive oil*
*2 teaspoons tapenade*
*2 slices of bresaola*
*6 stoned olives*
*1 plum tomato, sliced*
*1 tablespoon mixed peppers in*
*    tomato sauce*
*2 sprigs of fresh flat-leaf parsley*
*salt and freshly ground black pepper*

**1**   Toast the ciabatta on both sides.

**2**   Rub half a cut garlic clove over the toasted bread.

**3**   Drizzle the olive oil over the toast and spread with the tapenade.

**4**   Arrange the other ingredients on top, season and garnish with the parsley.

**WEIGHT WATCHERS TIP:** There are lots of ready-made antipasti available in jars. If you are using any of these (e.g. artichokes, sun-dried tomatoes or mushrooms), drain well before serving, and blot off as much oil as possible.

# CEVICHE

◆

*Serves 1 ◆ Preparation time 10 minutes + 1 hour marinating ◆ Freezing not recommended*
*I recently had a holiday in South America, where this dish is very common.*
*Don't be worried that you're eating raw fish, it actually 'cooks' in the acidity of the lime juice.*
*If you wish to make this for more people, augment the fish and avocado accordingly, but*
*only marginally increase the lime juice and chilli.*

Calories per serving: 130
Points per serving: 2

120 g (4 oz) firm-fleshed fish
   (e.g. monkfish, halibut, scallops or
   shelled prawns)
¼ small red or green chilli,
   de-seeded and sliced finely,
   or ¼ teaspoon chilli powder
½ red onion, chopped
grated zest and juice of 1 lime
⅛ avocado, chopped
1 tablespoon chopped fresh
   coriander
1 cup-shaped lettuce or radicchio
   leaf
salt and freshly ground black pepper

**1** Cut the fish in 1 cm (½-inch) cubes, rinse and pat dry, and then place in a non-metallic bowl.

**2** Add the chilli or chilli powder and onion. Stir in the lime zest and juice.

**3** Cover and leave in a cool place for one hour, stirring occasionally.

**4** Just before serving, stir in the avocado and coriander and season to taste. Spoon on to the salad leaf and enjoy.

# ASPARAGUS WITH BACON BOWS

◆

*Serves 2 ◆ Preparation time 5 minutes ◆ Cooking time 10 minutes ◆ Freezing not recommended*
*As asparagus comes into season for such a short time, it seems a shame to do anything more than*
*simply poach it. It could be served with the Yogurt Hollandaise (page 99),*
*or you could try Jane Grigson's idea of dipping individual spears,*
*like toast soldiers, into a soft-boiled egg.*

Calories per serving: 200
Points per serving: 4
Total Points per recipe: 8

*240 g (8 oz) asparagus*
*4 rashers of rindless streaky bacon*
*salt and freshly ground black pepper*

**1**   Trim the asparagus and cook them in a little water for 7 minutes.
(If you don't have an asparagus steamer, the best way to cook the spears
is in a frying-pan of water, as the spears can be laid flat without damaging
their delicate tips.) Drain carefully.

**2**   Meanwhile, stretch the bacon with the back of a knife. Preheat the grill
to hot.

**3**   Divide the spears into four bundles and tie each with a bacon bow.

**4**   Grill just long enough to crisp the bacon and reheat the asparagus.
Season and serve at once.

# PEPPER FRITTATA

◆

*Serves 6 ◆ Preparation time 10 minutes ◆ Cooking time 15 minutes ◆ Freezing not recommended*
*Even during the summer, a hot light meal is welcome, especially when it doesn't take long to cook.*
*This is a good dish for lunchtime. Serve with crusty fresh bread.*

Calories per serving: 155
Points per serving: 2½
Total Points per recipe: 15

*1 tablespoon olive oil*
*1 onion, chopped*
*1 garlic clove, sliced*
*3 peppers, assorted colours,*
   *de-seeded and cut in strips*
*6 eggs*
*60 g (2 oz) half-fat cheese, grated*
*salt and freshly ground black pepper*

**1**   Heat the oil in a frying-pan and stir-fry the onion, garlic and pepper
strips for 7–8 minutes, until the peppers are beginning to soften.

**2**   Beat the eggs in a small basin and add the cheese and seasoning.
Preheat the grill to medium.

**3**   Pour the egg mixture over the peppers; cook for 5 minutes over a
medium heat.

**4**   Put the pan under the grill until the top is browned.

**5**   Turn out on a plate before cutting in wedges.

**COOK'S NOTE:** You can substitute mushrooms or courgettes for the
peppers without effecting the Points.

# WATERCRESS AND COURGETTE MOUSSE

◆

*Serves 4 ◆ Preparation time 10 minutes ◆ Cooking time 30 minutes ◆ Freezing recommended*
*This cool green dish can be eaten with toast or crispbread and a mixed summer salad.*

Calories per serving: 105
Points per serving: 1½
Total Points per recipe: 6

1 teaspoon vegetable oil
240 g (8 oz) courgettes, grated
  coarsely
180 g (6 oz) Quark
½ teaspoon grated nutmeg
2 eggs, separated
1 bunch of watercress, chopped
salt and freshly ground black pepper

**1**  Preheat the oven to Gas Mark 4/180°C/350°F. Oil a 480 g (1 lb) loaf tin or four individual moulds.

**2**  Remove as much liquid as possible from the grated courgettes, by wrapping them in a clean tea towel and gently squeezing.

**3**  Mix the courgettes with the Quark, nutmeg, egg yolks and seasoning.

**4**  Whisk the egg whites until firm, then fold them into the courgette mixture.

**5**  Pour half the mixture into the prepared loaf tin or moulds.

**6**  Scatter the chopped watercress over the top, and then pour on the remaining courgette mixture.

**7**  Put the dish or dishes in a roasting tin half-filled with water (bain-marie) and place in the oven.

**8**  The mousse is ready when the mixture feels firm. It will take 30–40 minutes, depending on the size of the containers.

**9**  Allow to cool for 3 minutes before turning out on to a serving plate(s).

# MINTED CUCUMBER SOUP

◆

*Serves 1 ◆ Preparation time 5 minutes ◆ Freezing not recommended*
*When the sun is shining, this chilled soup is ideal. It takes no time at all to prepare and there is no slaving over a hot stove. You will remain cool as a cucumber!*

Calories per serving: 100
Points per serving: 1½

½ cucumber, cut in 1 cm
  (½-inch) cubes
150 g tub of low-fat natural yogurt
1 tablespoon chopped fresh mint,
  plus 1 mint leaf
1 tablespoon lemon juice
salt and freshly ground black pepper

**1**  Put the cucumber, yogurt, chopped mint and lemon juice in a food processor or liquidiser and blend for 1 minute.

**2**  Pour into a soup bowl, season to taste and garnish with a mint leaf.

MINTED CUCUMBER SOUP
VEAL ESCALOPES WITH ASPARAGUS RICE *(page 103)*

# WARM BEEF AND POTATO SALAD

◆

*Serves 4 ◆ Preparation time 10 minutes ◆ Cooking time 20 minutes ◆ Freezing not recommended*
*Use waxy new potatoes for this recipe (see page 193) and tender lean steak.*
*This is a good way to stretch a small grilling steak and I've found this a popular dish for picnics*
*and summer buffets.*

Calories per serving: 320
Points per serving: 5
Total Points per recipe: 20

*720 g (1½ lb) new potatoes,*
  *scrubbed*
*240 g (8 oz) french beans, topped*
  *and tailed*
*240 g (8 oz) lean steak (e.g. fillet,*
  *sirloin or rump)*
*1 bunch of watercress*
*420 g can of flageolet beans, rinsed*
  *and drained*
*2 tablespoons low-fat salad dressing*
*1 tablespoon wholegrain mustard*
*salt and freshly ground black pepper*

**1**  Cook the potatoes in lightly salted boiling water for 20 minutes, adding the french beans 5 minutes before the end.

**2**  Drain and rinse the vegetables in cold water. Drain again.

**3**  Meanwhile, grill the steak to your taste and cut in strips.

**4**  Slice the warm potatoes and cut the beans in half.

**5**  Mix together the potatoes, french beans, steak, watercress and flageolet beans in a large bowl.

**6**  Whisk together the dressing and mustard and toss into the salad, with a little salt and plenty of freshly ground black pepper.

# SALMON WITH YOGURT HOLLANDAISE

*Serves 4 ◆ Preparation time 5 minutes ◆ Cooking time 20 minutes ◆ Freezing recommended for salmon if it has not already been frozen*

*Fresh salmon is an integral part of the British summer and hollandaise is the classic sauce to serve with it. This low-fat version of the sauce is delicious.*

Calories per serving: 250
Points per serving: 4½
Total Points per recipe: 18

*4 × 120 g (4 oz) salmon steaks*

*1 teaspoon vegetable oil*

**FOR THE SAUCE:**

*150 g tub of low-fat natural yogurt*

*2 egg yolks*

*1 teaspoon cornflour*

*1 teaspoon wholegrain or Dijon mustard*

*1 teaspoon lemon juice*

*salt and freshly ground black pepper*

*4 spring onions, to garnish*

**1** Set a heatproof basin over a pan of simmering water, or use a double boiler, if you have one.

**2** Whisk together the yogurt, egg yolks and cornflour until thick enough to coat a spoon. This will take about 8 minutes.

**3** Remove from the heat and stir in the mustard, lemon juice and seasoning. Leave to cool. Preheat the grill to medium.

**4** Brush the salmon steaks with oil and season with freshly ground black pepper.

**5** Grill for about 4 minutes on each side.

**6** Serve the steaks with a spoonful of sauce on top and garnish with the spring onions.

**COOK'S NOTE:** Use the leftover egg whites to make the Strawberry and Raspberry Mousse (page 104) for a perfect end to this special meal.

# CHICKEN STIR-FRY WITH RICE NOODLES

◆

*Serves 4 ◆ Preparation time 15 minutes ◆ Cooking time 10 minutes ◆ Freezing not recommended*
*Nobody wants to spend time in the kitchen when the weather is warm, so a stir-fry is a quick*
*solution. Prepare the ingredients in the morning when the weather is cool and then simply*
*throw them into the pan 10 minutes before you're ready to eat!*
*You can substitute dried herbs for fresh if you prefer.*

Calories per serving: 245
Points per serving: 5½
Total Points per recipe: 22

*240 g (8 oz) rice noodles*

*1 tablespoon vegetable oil*

*2 boneless, skinless chicken breasts,*
*  cut in strips*

*2 carrots, cut in matchsticks*

*1 onion, chopped*

*2.5 cm (1-inch) piece of fresh root*
*  ginger, chopped finely*

*120 g (4 oz) button mushrooms,*
*  sliced*

*2 garlic cloves, sliced thinly*

*240 g (8 oz) mangetout, topped*
*  and tailed*

*1 tablespoon dry sherry (optional)*

*1 teaspoon light soy sauce*

*1 tablespoon chopped fresh*
*  coriander, to garnish*

**1**  Cook the rice noodles according to the packet instructions. Drain.

**2**  Heat the oil in a wok or large frying-pan and stir-fry the chicken for 2 minutes. Remove from the pan.

**3**  Add the carrots, onion and ginger to the pan and stir-fry for 3 minutes. Stir in the mushrooms and garlic and cook for 1 more minute.

**4**  Return the chicken to the pan with the mangetout, sherry (if using) and soy sauce and cook for 3 minutes.

**5**  Stir in the drained noodles, season to taste, and serve the stir-fry in a large warm bowl, garnished with the coriander.

CHICKEN STIR-FRY WITH RICE NOODLES
PINEAPPLE BOATS *(page 105)*

# SEAFOOD PASTA

◆

*Serves 4 ◆ Preparation time 10 minutes ◆ Cooking time 15 minutes ◆ Freezing recommended*
*Spinach pasta with prawns looks and tastes great, but you can use pasta shells instead.*
*This seaside dish will whet your appetite for summer holidays to come.*

Calories per serving: 305
Points per serving: 4
Total Points per recipe: 16

*240 g (8 oz) green noodles, pasta*
*shapes or a mixture of both*

*1 tablespoon olive oil*

*2 garlic cloves, sliced*

*120 g (4 oz) button mushrooms*

*4 tablespoons very-low-fat fromage*
*frais*

*1 tablespoon tomato purée*

*240 g (8 oz) cooked peeled prawns*
*or mixed seafood or salmon*

*1 tablespoon chopped fresh parsley*

*salt and freshly ground black pepper*

*4 teaspoons freshly grated parmesan*
*cheese, to serve*

**1**  Cook the pasta according to the packet instructions – fresh pasta will take much less time than dried – and drain well.

**2**  Heat the oil in a shallow pan and cook the garlic over a low heat until softened.

**3**  Add the mushrooms and cook for 2 minutes.

**4**  Stir in the fromage frais, tomato purée, seafood and parsley.

**5**  Season to taste and add the cooked pasta. Toss together until heated through.

**6**  Sprinkle each serving with a teaspoon of parmesan.

**COOK'S NOTE:** Prawns and pasta make a good summer salad too. Cook the pasta and rinse in cold water. Mix together with cooked peeled prawns, chopped parsley and low-Calorie mayonnaise.

# RACK OF LAMB WITH BEANS

◆

*Serves 6 ◆ Preparation time 5 minutes ◆ Cooking time 30–45 minutes ◆ Freezing not recommended*

Calories per serving: 440
Points per serving: 6
Total Points per recipe: 36

*2 racks of new season's lamb*

*2 garlic cloves, sliced*

*2 sprigs of fresh rosemary*

*1 onion, chopped*

*2 × 420 g cans of haricot or*
   *flageolet beans*

*2 tomatoes, skinned and chopped*

*150 g tub of Quark*

*salt and freshly ground black pepper*

**1**   Preheat the oven to Gas Mark 7/220°C/425°F.

**2**   Trim the lamb of fat. Insert the garlic slices and rosemary under the skin of the lamb. Place the lamb on a roasting rack and roast on the top shelf of the oven for 30 minutes for pink lamb, and 45 minutes if you prefer it well cooked.

**3**   Drain off the fat, reserving the meat juices and 1 tablespoon of fat.

**4**   Fry the onion in the reserved fat for 5 minutes. Rinse and drain the beans. Add them, with the tomatoes, Quark and any meat juices, to the onion. Season well.

**5**   Carve the lamb into cutlets and serve on a hot platter, with the beans.

# VEAL ESCALOPES WITH ASPARAGUS RICE

◆

*Serves 2 ◆ Preparation time 10 minutes ◆ Cooking time 15 minutes ◆ Freezing recommended*
*It is often possible to buy off-cuts of asparagus, which are ideal for mixing with other ingredients.*

Calories per serving: 370
Points per serving: 6½
Total Points per recipe: 13

*1 sachet of boil-in-the-bag rice*

*1 tablespoon vegetable oil*

*1 small red pepper, de-seeded and*
   *cut in 1 cm (½-inch) squares*

*120 g (4 oz) asparagus off-cuts, cut*
   *in 2.5 cm (1-inch) lengths*

*1 tablespoon dried breadcrumbs*

*2 × 90 g (3 oz) veal escalopes or*
   *pork steaks*

*salt and freshly ground black pepper*

*2 lemon wedges, to serve*

**1**   Cook the rice according to the packet instructions and drain well.

**2**   Heat the oil and stir-fry the pepper and asparagus for 5 minutes. Preheat the grill to medium.

**3**   Stir in the rice and season to taste.

**4**   Press the breadcrumbs on to both sides of the meat.

**5**   Grill the meat until golden on both sides.

**6**   Serve with the asparagus rice and lemon wedges.

# STRAWBERRY AND RASPBERRY MOUSSE

♦

*Serves 4 ♦ Preparation time 15 minutes ♦ Freezing recommended*
*The first of the soft summer fruits start to come into the shops this month. You may be lucky*
*enough to grow or pick your own. Because the fruit is whizzed to a purée in this recipe, there*
*is no point in using the best quality (although you may like to keep one or two good berries*
*to decorate the top). You can use any combination of fruit in this mousse –*
*just choose a complementary jelly flavour.*

Calories per serving: 65
Points per serving: ½
Total Points per recipe: 2

*120 g (4 oz) ripe strawberries*
*120 g (4 oz) raspberries*
*1 packet of sugar-free strawberry or*
*    raspberry jelly*
*2 egg whites*

**1**  Blend the fruit in a processor or liquidiser, or rub it through a sieve.

**2**  Make up the jelly with 150 ml (¼ pint) of hot water.

**3**  Stir until dissolved and then add the purée and water to make 450 ml (¾ pint) of jelly.

**4**  Whisk the egg whites in a large bowl until stiff.

**5**  Fold in the jelly mixture and pour the mousse into a pretty glass bowl, or a jelly mould, or into individual moulds or glass dishes.

**6**  Leave in a cool place to set, and then turn out on a plate to serve (if using a mould).

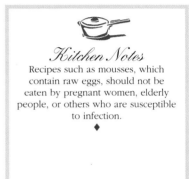

*Kitchen Notes*
Recipes such as mousses, which
contain raw eggs, should not be
eaten by pregnant women, elderly
people, or others who are susceptible
to infection.

♦

# PINEAPPLE BOATS

◆

*Serves 4 ◆ Preparation time 10 minutes ◆ Freezing not recommended*
*Fresh pineapple is so delicious. This fruit salad makes full use of the fruit.*

Calories per serving: 80
Points per serving: 1
Total Points per recipe: 4

ⓥ

*1 pineapple*
*120 g (4 oz) small strawberries,*
*  hulled*
*4 tablespoons very-low-fat fromage*
*  frais*

**TO GARNISH:**

*half a medium-sized orange*
*4 sprigs of fresh mint*

**1**   Remove the woody stem of the pineapple and cut it in quarters lengthways, retaining the leaves.

**2**   Using a sharp knife, trim away the core and discard.

**3**   Cut away the remaining flesh from the skin, and chop it into bite-sized cubes.

**4**   Mix the pineapple chunks with the strawberries and fromage frais, and divide between the hollowed-out pineapple skins.

**5**   Cut four thin slices from the half-orange. Twist the orange slices and use one to decorate each 'boat'. Garnish with the sprigs of mint.

*Kitchen Notes*
A pineapple often looks good from the outside but is a disappointment when cut open. To tell if it fresh and ripe, look at the leaves. They should be lush and green, not brown and shrivelled. If the pineapple is ripe, the leaves in the centre of the tuft should pull out easily.

◆

# July

The barbecue and *al fresco* dining season starts in earnest this month, and there is no healthier way of cooking than barbecue grilling, which allows excess fat to drip away. Barbecued food accompanied by a fresh salad and some crusty brown bread is an ideal balanced meal. A well-flavoured marinade will tenderise meat as well as adding flavour. The recipe for Chicken Kebabs (page 114) can be used for other types of meat as well.

Home-grown cherries should be plentiful this month, and if you can buy or pick Morello cherries, their tart flavour works well in sauces and preserves. The soft fruit season continues and British beans, peas and courgettes should be available now. Steamed lightly, stir-fried, or served raw in salads, these summer vegetables are healthy and delicious.

The best of the summer fruits and vegetables from the Mediterranean are beginning to appear in the shops now – aubergines, sweet peppers, plum tomatoes and melons are all the tastier for having ripened under Mediterranean sun.

COLD CURRIED CHICKEN *(page 115)*
FRENCH BEAN AND TOMATO SALAD *(page 109)*
CHERRY AND MUESLI SUNDAE *(page 121)*

# SOFT FRUIT CORNUCOPIA

*Serves 2 ♦ Preparation time 5 minutes ♦ Freezing not recommended*
*A simple fresh fruit salad is a quick and delicious way to start your day. The croissant makes*
*it rather special. A cornucopia is another word for the mythical horn of plenty, which was*
*always full of good things, and the croissant shape is reminiscent of this.*

Calories per serving: 165
Points per serving: 3
Total Points per recipe: 6
Ⓥ

*1 fresh well-shaped croissant*
*180 g (6 oz) mixed soft fruit*

**1** Cut the croissant in half and place on two dessert plates.
**2** Arrange the fruit so that it appears to tumble out of the croissant.

# MIXED BEAN SALAD

*Serves 4 ♦ Preparation time 10 minutes ♦ Freezing not recommended*
*Round, bowl-shaped leaves make good edible containers for salads. I like the bright pink colour of*
*radicchio but Iceberg will do very nicely, if you prefer. You could also use chicory leaves*
*and arrange them like flower petals for each person.*

Calories per serving: 145
Points per serving: 2
Total Points per recipe: 8
Ⓥ

*215 g can of red kidney beans,*
  *rinsed and drained*
*420 g can of flageolet beans, rinsed*
  *and drained*
*220 g can of haricot beans, rinsed*
  *and drained*
*3 tablespoons low-fat vinaigrette*
  *dressing*
*1 tablespoon chopped fresh chives*
*4 bowl-shaped lettuce leaves*

**1** Mix the beans together and toss them in the vinaigrette and chives.
**2** Arrange the leaves on individual plates and divide the bean salad
between them.

**VARIATIONS:** The key ingredient in this salad is the edible salad bowl.
Otherwise, use any salad vegetables you like. Use fewer beans and mix
in some grated carrot or cherry tomatoes. Or omit one variety of bean
altogether and use canned sweetcorn.

# FRENCH BEAN AND TOMATO SALAD

◆

*Serves 2 ◆ Preparation time 10 minutes ◆ Cooking time 5 minutes*
*Freezing not recommended*
*Serve this lovely colourful salad for a summer meal, along with some crusty bread.*

Calories per serving: 125
Points per serving: 2
Total Points per recipe: 4
Ⓥ if using vegetarian cheese

*180 g (6 oz) french beans, topped*
*    and tailed*
*4 plum tomatoes*
*2 tablespoons tomato juice*
*2 teaspoons lemon juice*
*1 tablespoon chopped fresh parsley*
*30 g (1 oz) parmesan cheese,*
*    shaved or grated*
*salt and freshly ground black pepper*

**1**  Snap the beans in half, if very long, and plunge them into boiling water. Cook for 5 minutes. Drain and rinse immediately in cold water. Drain again and transfer to a serving bowl.

**2**  Skin the tomatoes (see below) and slice them thinly crossways. Add them to the drained beans.

**3**  Mix together the tomato juice, lemon juice, parsley and seasoning.

**4**  Pour the dressing over the salad and top with the shaved or grated cheese.

*Kitchen Notes*
The easiest way to skin tomatoes is to put them in a basin and pour *boiling* water over them to cover. Leave for 2 minutes and then drain. The skin will peel off easily. An alternative method, if you have a gas cooker, is to spear the tomato on a fork and hold it in the blue part of the flame on the gas ring. When the skin begins to blister, remove from the heat and leave until cool enough to handle. Peel off the skin.

◆

# POTTED SALMON SANDWICH

♦

*Serves 1 ♦ Preparation time 5 minutes + chilling ♦*
*Freezing recommended without salad ingredients*
*You could substitute trout in this recipe if you prefer. Potted fish has a lovely, melt-in-your-mouth*
*texture and the taste is superb. You can keep this in the refrigerator for up to 4 days.*

Calories per serving: 540
Points per serving: 5

*60 g (2 oz) cooked salmon*

*a pinch of ground nutmeg, mace or*
  *Chinese five-spice powder*

*1 tablespoon very-low-fat natural*
  *fromage frais*

*30 g (1 oz) butter*

*1 teaspoon lemon juice*

*1 ciabatta roll, split in half*

*2 lettuce leaves, shredded*

*½ small courgette, sliced*

*salt and freshly ground black pepper*

**1**  Mix the salmon with the spice and fromage frais. Season to taste and pack into a small ramekin.

**2**  Melt the butter and pour it over the top.

**3**  Refrigerate until chilled, and then remove the hardened disk of butter and mix the lemon juice in with the salmon.

**4**  Spread the salmon on one side of the roll and top with the lettuce and courgette. Season and top with the other half of the roll.

**COOK'S NOTE:** Sandwiches can be made in batches and frozen individually – they don't take long to defrost. Don't freeze salad ingredients, but add them fresh to thawed sandwiches.

*Kitchen Notes*
'Potting' is a way of preserving cooked fish, meat or cheese. The butter topping makes an airtight seal once chilled, and can be removed before eating. Try potting canned drained fish or cooked chopped beef. Mix them with some fat-free fromage frais and your favourite herbs or spices.

♦

# TUNA PÂTÉ ON TOAST

◆

*Serves 4 ◆ Preparation time 5 minutes ◆ Cooking time 5 minutes ◆ Freezing recommended*
*This simple snack could be made with most canned fish. It's a good idea to buy fish that is*
*canned in water or brine rather than in oil.*

Calories per serving: 250
Points per serving: 4½
Total Points per recipe: 18

4 slices of wholemeal bread
200 g can of tuna in water or brine
120 g (4 oz) low-fat spread
1 tablespoon horseradish sauce
8 stoned green or black olives,
    chopped (optional)
freshly ground black pepper
**TO GARNISH:**
8 cucumber slices
4 lemon slices
4 sprigs of fresh parsley

**1**  Toast the bread on both sides and keep it warm.

**2**  Drain the tuna and beat together with the low-fat spread, horseradish and olives, if using. Season to taste with pepper (you may not need any salt if using olives and/or brined tuna).

**3**  Spread thickly on the toast and top each slice with two pieces of cucumber, a slice of lemon and a parsley sprig.

# MELON, CHICKEN AND MINT COCKTAIL

*Serves 2 ◆ Preparation time 10 minutes ◆ Freezing not recommended*
*Melon goes well with chicken and, once the flesh is scooped out, small melon halves make the*
*perfect serving dish. Use whatever strength curry paste you prefer, or leave it out altogether.*

Calories per serving: 150
Points per serving: 4
Total Points per recipe: 8

1 small melon
120 g (4 oz) cooked chicken, skin
    removed
1 tablespoon chopped fresh mint,
    plus 2 sprigs, to garnish
150 g tub of low-fat natural yogurt
1 teaspoon curry paste (optional)
salt and freshly ground black pepper

**1**  Halve the melon, discard the seeds and scoop out the flesh. Chop the flesh and put in a bowl, reserving the melon halves. Alternatively, use a melon baller.

**2**  Chop the chicken into bite-sized pieces and add them to the melon.

**3**  Blend in the mint, yogurt and curry paste, if using.

**4**  Season to taste and spoon the mixture into the melon halves.

**5**  Refrigerate until serving and then garnish with mint sprigs.

**VARIATION:** Replace the cooked chicken with prawns and reduce the Points per serving to 2½ or use ham and reduce the Points to 3 per serving.

# PASTA SALADE NIÇOISE

◆

*Serves 4 ◆ Preparation time 10 minutes ◆ Cooking time 20 minutes ◆ Freezing not recommended*
*This is simply a salade Niçoise served hot, with pasta instead of the traditional lettuce.*

Calories per serving: 295
Points per serving: 3
Total Points per recipe: 12

*180 g (6 oz) pasta spirals*

*120 g (4 oz) french beans, topped,*
*  tailed and cut in half*

*2 plum tomatoes, skinned (see*
*  page 109) and sliced*

*1 green pepper, de-seeded and sliced*

*100 g can of tuna in brine, drained*

*50 g can of anchovy fillets, drained*
*  and chopped, with oil reserved*

*2 eggs, hard-boiled*

*8 stoned black olives, chopped*

*2 tablespoons lemon juice*

*salt and freshly ground black pepper*

*1 tablespoon chopped fresh parsley,*
*  to serve*

**1**  Cook the pasta according to the packet instructions and, at the same time, steam the beans in a sieve or colander over the pasta pan.

**2**  Place the sliced tomatoes, green pepper, drained tuna and chopped anchovy fillets in a bowl.

**3**  Shell and quarter the hard-boiled eggs, and add them to the bowl, with the chopped olives.

**4**  Drain the pasta and then return it to the pan, with the beans and the ingredients in the bowl.

**5**  Stir in the reserved anchovy oil and the lemon juice, and toss over a low heat until heated through.

**6**  Season well and serve sprinkled with chopped parsley.

POTTED SALMON SANDWICH *(page 110)*
PASTA SALADE NIÇOISE

# CHICKEN KEBABS

◆

*Serves 4 ◆ Preparation time 10 minutes + 1 hour marinating ◆ Cooking time 10 minutes ◆*
*Freezing recommended*
*This is the ideal recipe for summer barbecues and, if the weather is inclement, simply cook the*
*kebabs under the grill. Make sure that the chicken is cooked thoroughly. The danger with*
*barbecuing is that one can cook the food too quickly on the outside and leave the inside still raw.*
*You could serve these on a bed of plain boiled rice or inside toasted pitta.*

Calories per serving: 130
Points per serving: 2
Total Points per recipe: 8

*240 g (8 oz) boneless, skinless*
   *chicken breast, cut in bite-sized*
   *pieces*
*½ red pepper, de-seeded and cut in*
   *2.5 cm (1-inch) squares*
*½ green pepper, de-seeded and cut*
   *in 2.5 cm (1-inch) squares*
*1 onion, quartered*
*8 mushrooms*
*1 tablespoon olive oil*
*1 tablespoon lemon juice*
*2 teaspoons chopped fresh herbs or*
   *1 teaspoon dried mixed herbs*
*salt and freshly ground black pepper*

**1**  Place the chicken, peppers, onion quarters and mushrooms in a bowl.

**2**  Mix together the oil, lemon juice and herbs and pour over the kebab ingredients.

**3**  Season well and leave to marinate for at least 1 hour.

**4**  Preheat the barbecue or grill.

**5**  Divide the ingredients into four and thread on to skewers, alternating the ingredients. Reserve any remaining marinade.

**6**  Grill or barbecue the kebabs for 10 minutes, turning frequently and basting with the marinade.

# COLD CURRIED CHICKEN

◆

*Serves 4 ◆ Preparation time 10 minutes ◆ Cooking time 45 minutes + at least 1 hour chilling ◆*
*Freezing recommended*

*This is a variation on that ever-popular summer dish, Coronation Chicken. It would be ideal for*
*a buffet or relaxed supper with friends. Although it can be eaten as soon as it has chilled,*
*I find the flavour really improves if it is refrigerated overnight.*

Calories per serving: 190
Points per serving: 3
Total Points per recipe: 12

*2 boneless, skinless chicken breasts*

*½ tablespoon plain flour, seasoned*

*1 tablespoon vegetable oil*

*2 onions, chopped*

*1 tablespoon curry powder*

*1 teaspoon ground cinnamon*

*1 teaspoon ground ginger*

*1 tablespoon mango chutney*

*1 cooking apple, peeled, quartered*
  *and sliced*

*150 ml (¼ pint) water*

*150 ml (¼ pint) skimmed milk*

*150 g tub of low-fat natural yogurt*

*1 tablespoon chopped fresh*
  *coriander*

*salt and freshly ground black pepper*

**1**   Coat the chicken breasts in seasoned flour.

**2**   Heat the oil in a pan and brown the chicken on both sides, until golden.

**3**   Remove from the pan and add the onions, spices, chutney and apple.

**4**   Cook for 5 more minutes, and then add the water and milk.

**5**   Bring to the boil and then reduce to a simmer. Put the chicken back into the pan and cook for 30 minutes.

**6**   Remove the chicken from the pan and cut into bite-sized pieces.

**7**   Stir the chicken back in and add the yogurt and coriander. Season to taste.

**8**   Transfer to a serving dish and refrigerate for at least 1 hour before serving.

# TABBOULEH WITH CURRANTS

◆

*Serves 4 ♦ Preparation time 10 minutes + 10 minutes soaking + chilling ♦ Freezing recommended*
*This salad originates in the Middle East, and is the traditional accompaniment for many lamb*
*dishes. Serve it with grilled lamb chops or chicken kebabs. It can also be enjoyed on its own.*
*Bulgar wheat is a starchy grain and has the advantage of needing no cooking, merely soaking.*

Calories per serving: 195
Points per serving: 1½
Total Points per recipe: 6
(V)

*150 g (5 oz) bulgar wheat*

*6 spring onions, sliced*

*60 g (2 oz) currants*

*2 tomatoes*

*2 tablespoons chopped fresh parsley*

*1 tablespoon chopped fresh mint*

*4 tablespoons low-fat vinaigrette*
  *dressing*

*grated zest and juice of 1 lemon*

**1**  Cover the bulgar wheat with cold water and leave to soak for at least
10 minutes, or until the grains swell to twice their original size.

**2**  Drain and transfer to a serving bowl.

**3**  Add the spring onions and currants.

**4**  Skin the tomatoes (see page 109), and then de-seed and chop them.
Add to the bowl with the parsley and mint.

**5**  Blend the vinaigrette with the grated zest and lemon juice and stir it
into the salad until well mixed. Refrigerate and serve chilled.

# PLAICE WITH HERB SAUCE

◆

*Serves 4 ◆ Preparation time 5 minutes ◆ Cooking time 10 minutes ◆ Freezing not recommended*
*Fresh herbs are at their best in summer and add flavour to delicate foods without*
*overpowering them. This herb sauce would go well with any white fish. Plaice and lemon sole*
*cook very quickly and are relatively inexpensive.*

Calories per serving: 135
Points per serving: 2½
Total Points per recipe: 10

*4 plaice or lemon sole fillets,*
*skinned*

*1 teaspoon vegetable oil*

*3 tablespoons chopped mixed fresh*
*herbs (e.g. parsley, dill, chervil,*
*chives, fennel, tarragon and*
*marjoram)*

*250 ml tub of very-low-fat fromage*
*frais*

*4 lemon wedges*

*salt and freshly ground black pepper*

**1** Preheat the grill.

**2** Brush the fillets with the oil and season well.

**3** Grill the fish for about 3 minutes on both sides

**4** Stir together the herbs and fromage frais and season to taste.

**5** Serve the fish and sauce separately, accompanied by the lemon wedges.

# GRILLED SALMON WITH FRESH TOMATO SALSA

◆

*Serves 2 ◆ Preparation time 10 minutes ◆ Cooking time 5 minutes ◆ Freezing not recommended*
*Salmon is still considered a luxury but now that it is farmed, the price is much more affordable.*
*It is an oily fish containing omega-3 fatty acids, which may guard against cholesterol deposits.*
*Fresh tomatoes are at their best at this time of year, and this sauce is refreshing*
*as well as flavoursome. It is called a salsa in Mexican cooking.*

Calories per serving: 150
Points per serving: 3
Total Points per recipe: 6

*2 × 90 g (3 oz) salmon fillets*

**FOR THE SALSA:**

*2 tomatoes*

*1 green chilli*

*1 small onion, chopped finely*

*1 teaspoon lemon juice*

*1 tablespoon chopped fresh*
  *coriander*

*salt and freshly ground black pepper*

**1**  Season the salmon on both sides and preheat the grill to medium.

**2**  Skin the tomatoes (see page 109). Quarter the tomatoes and remove the seeds. Chop the flesh finely

**3**  De-seed and slice the chilli thinly.

**4**  Mix the tomato, chilli, onion, lemon juice and coriander. Season to taste.

**5**  Grill the salmon for 2–3 minutes on each side.

**6**  Serve immediately, with the salsa.

**COOK'S NOTES:** Take great care when handling chillies not to touch your eyes or nose until you've washed your hands thoroughly.

Boiled new potatoes would go very well with this dish. A medium-sized portion is 2 Points.

# SUMMER POTATO CASSEROLE

♦

*Serves 4 ♦ Preparation time 10 minutes ♦ Cooking time 30–45 minutes ♦ Freezing recommended*
*Once the casserole has gone into the oven, it needs no attention and will keep quite well in*
*a low oven for some time. The flavour of the juniper berries adds a refreshing sharpness.*
*(Juniper is used to give gin its distinctive flavour and the berries can be found*
*in the spice section of your supermarket.)*

Calories per serving: 105
Points per serving: 1½
Total Points per recipe: 6

1 onion, chopped

2 garlic cloves, chopped finely

20 juniper berries, crushed
  (optional)

480 g (1 lb) plum tomatoes, skinned
  (see page 109) and sliced

1 tablespoon chopped fresh thyme

480 g (1 lb) potatoes, scrubbed
  and sliced

150 ml (¼ pint) vegetable stock

salt and freshly ground black pepper

**1**   Preheat the oven to Gas Mark 6/200°C/400°F.

**2**   Divide the ingredients, except for the stock, in two.

**3**   Put half the onion, garlic and juniper berries (if using) in a
casserole. Season.

**4**   Cover with a layer of sliced tomatoes and half the thyme. Season again.

**5**   Add a layer of potatoes.

**6**   Repeat the layers with the remaining ingredients, and pour the stock
over the casserole.

**7**   Bake, uncovered, for 30–45 minutes.

**VARIATION:** Add a layer of chopped green peppers with the first layer of
potato. This will not add any Points.

# KISSEL

◆

*Serves 2 ◆ Preparation time 10 minutes ◆ Cooking time 15 minutes ◆ Freezing not recommended*
*This Scandinavian dish is ideally made when all the soft fruits are at their best. If you don't have*
*arrowroot, use cornflour which will thicken the juice but give a cloudy appearance.*

Calories per serving: 95
Points per serving: 1½
Total Points per recipe: 3

Ⓥ

*1 orange*
*180 g (6 oz) mixed blackcurrants*
*    and redcurrants, stalks removed*
*120 g (4 oz) raspberries*
*120 g (4 oz) small strawberries*
*2 teaspoons arrowroot*
*artificial sweetener, to taste*

**1**  Peel the zest from half the orange and shred finely. Reserve. Squeeze the juice into a small pan.

**2**  Put the currants in with the juice, bring to the boil and then simmer for 10 minutes.

**3**  Drain the currants, reserving the juice, and place them in a bowl with the raspberries and strawberries.

**4**  Return the juice to the pan, add 2 tablespoons of water and blend in the arrowroot.

**5**  Bring to the boil, stirring constantly, until the juice thickens.

**6**  Add artificial sweetener to taste, and pour over the fruit.

**7**  Garnish with the shredded orange zest and leave until cold.

# CHERRY AND MUESLI SUNDAE

◆

*Serves 1 ◆ Preparation time 10 minutes ◆ Freezing not recommended*
*Choose luscious dark cherries and unsweetened muesli for this easy-to-prepare dish. Any of the*
*summer berries or soft fruits could be treated in the same way.*
*A cherry stoner would come in handy.*

Calories per serving: 270
Points per serving: 3½
V

120 g (4 oz) ripe cherries
1 tablespoon cranberry and
   raspberry juice
2 tablespoons muesli
1 scoop of Weight Watchers vanilla
   ice cream or frozen yogurt

**1**   Keep one stemmed cherry for decoration. Remove the stems and stone the rest of the cherries and put them in the bottom of a sundae glass, along with any cherry juices and the cranberry-raspberry juice.

**2**   Spoon the muesli over the top.

**3**   Add the ice-cream and top with the reserved cherry.

**COOK'S NOTE:** Cranberry and raspberry juice is readily available in cardboard cartons and is long-life until opened. Make a jelly with the remaining juice, by using a sachet of sugar-free strawberry or blackcurrant jelly crystals.

# August

This is the most popular time for taking holidays and trips to the country or seaside. Pack up picnic salads in plastic boxes or, if you prefer sandwiches, then try the Pan Bagnat (page 133), a traditional sandwich from the south of France. Stoned fruits like peaches and nectarines are at their best now, and these make an ideal dessert. Melon is a refreshing starter, whether on its own or served with thinly sliced ham. Be adventurous and try out new breads which will add variety to sandwiches, making them something rather more special than the sliced-loaf variety. Pitta bread seems as though it were especially created for sandwich fillings, and is available in white and brown, and in small rounds as well as the larger oval ones.

British salad vegetables are at their best this month, and the range of lettuces is astounding. The apple season is just beginning now, with the early variety called Discovery. Try them sliced and added to green lettuce salads.

The game season also starts this month and game birds are naturally low in fat and therefore very healthy. Venison can be used in a similar way to beef, its flavour being just a little stronger.

SPICED BEEF PATTIES *(page 132)*
STUFFED TOMATOES *(page 125)*
PEACH AND RASPBERRY CRISP *(page 137)*

# BACON AND TOMATO OMELETTE

◆

*Serves 1* ◆ *Preparation time 5 minutes* ◆ *Cooking time 5 minutes* ◆ *Freezing not recommended*
*No wonder omelettes are the ideal food for one. They are so quick to make and the variations*
*are endless. I find that the addition of a little water to the egg makes a really light omelette.*
*With fresh bread or toast, an omelette is equally suitable for a light meal as for breakfast.*

Calories per serving: 160
Points per serving: 4

*1 rasher of lean bacon, with rind*
*    removed, chopped coarsely*
*1 tomato, chopped coarsely*
*1 egg*
*salt and freshly ground black pepper*

**1**   Heat a small, non-stick omelette pan and add the bacon.

**2**   When the bacon is sizzling, add the tomato.

**3**   Beat the egg with 1 tablespoon of water and season well.

**4**   Pour the egg into the pan and, using a palette knife, slowly draw the set edges into the middle, allowing the liquid egg to run towards the edges.

**5**   When set, fold the omelette in half and serve on a warm plate.

**VARIATIONS**: Add mushrooms and strips of pepper, or sliced, cooked asparagus. This will not add any Points.

# STUFFED TOMATOES

◆

*Serves 2 ◆ Preparation time 10 minutes ◆ Freezing not recommended*
*This easily prepared light meal could also be part of a summer buffet or picnic.*

Calories per serving: 230
Points per serving: 2¹/₂
Total Points per recipe: 5

2 large beef tomatoes or 4 medium-
    sized tomatoes
150 g (5 oz) low-fat cottage cheese
100 g can of tuna in water, drained
    and flaked
1 tablespoon chopped fresh chives
1 teaspoon horseradish sauce
2 fresh basil sprigs
salt and freshly ground black pepper
2 slices of french bread, toasted,
    to serve

**1**  Cut a slice from the top of each tomato and reserve.

**2**  Carefully scoop out the tomato seeds and flesh and stand the tomato shells upside down in a bowl to drain.

**3**  Mix together the cottage cheese, tuna, chives and horseradish sauce with the tomato flesh and any juices. Season to taste.

**4**  Spoon the mixture into the tomato shells and garnish each with a basil sprig before replacing the lid.

**5**  Serve the tomatoes on top of the toasted french bread.

# LETTUCE AND POTATO SOUP

◆

*Serves 4 ◆ Preparation time 10 minutes ◆ Cooking time 25 minutes ◆ Freezing not recommended*
*If you have any lettuces on hand which have bolted (started to go to seed), this soup is a good*
*way to use them up. You could also use the tougher outside leaves of a lettuce, which you might*
*otherwise discard. I've suggested parsley, but you can use whatever herbs you have.*

Calories per serving: 105
Points per serving: 1
Total Points per recipe: 4

1 large lettuce
1 tablespoon vegetable oil
1 small onion, chopped
1 potato, peeled and sliced
500 ml (³/₄ pint) vegetable stock
500 ml (³/₄ pint) skimmed milk
1 tablespoon chopped fresh parsley
salt and freshly ground black pepper

**1**  Wash and drain the lettuce leaves.

**2**  Heat the oil in a saucepan and gently fry the onion without browning.

**3**  Add the potato and lettuce and cook, covered, for 5 minutes.

**4**  Add the stock and milk, and simmer for 20 minutes, or until the potato softens.

**5**  Stir in the parsley and whizz in a food processor or liquidiser.

**6**  Season to taste and reheat before serving, if necessary.

# GAZPACHO SOUP

◆

*Serves 4 ◆ Preparation time 15 minutes ◆ Freezing recommended without the garnishes*
*This chilled Spanish tomato soup is made more substantial by a selection of garnishes.*
*A liquidiser or food processor is needed to make the soup.*

Calories per serving: 100
Points per serving: 1
Total Points per recipe: 4

Ⓥ

*1 onion, cut in half*

*1 garlic clove*

*1 green pepper, de-seeded and cut*
  *in half*

*240 g (8 oz) tomatoes*

*1 cucumber, cut in half*

*6 thin slices of french stick*

*450 ml (¾ pint) tomato juice*

*juice of 1 lemon*

*6 drops of Tabasco sauce, or to taste*

*salt*

**1**  In a food processor or liquidiser, blend together half the onion, the garlic, half the green pepper, all but one tomato, and half the cucumber. Strain into a bowl and refrigerate.

**2**  Prepare the garnishes: finely chop the remaining onion half, chop the pepper and cucumber and toast the bread slowly until crisp.

**3**  Just before serving, stir the tomato juice, lemon juice and Tabasco sauce into the soup. Season to taste with salt only.

**4**  Serve the soup surrounded by small bowls of the garnishes.

# TANDOORI CHICKEN AND CARROT SALAD

◆

*Serves 1 ◆ Preparation time 10 minutes + 1 hour chilling ◆ Freezing not recommended*
*A few flavoured and ready-cooked chicken pieces make the basis of a quick-and-easy spicy salad.*
*Serve with a small naan bread or a couple of papads.*

Calories per serving: 220
Points per serving: 3

*3 cubes (120 g/4 oz) ready-cooked*
  *tandoori chicken*

*1 carrot, peeled and grated*

*2 tablespoons low-fat natural yogurt*

*1 tablespoon lemon juice*

*1 teaspoon chopped fresh mint*

*salt and freshly ground black pepper*

**1**  Slice the chicken and toss together with the rest of the ingredients. Season to taste.

**2**  Chill for 1 hour to let the flavours blend before serving.

# CITRUS CHICKEN SALAD

◆

*Serves 2 ◆ Preparation time 10 minutes ◆ Cooking time 20 minutes + 4 hours chilling ◆*
*Freezing recommended*

*Because the cooked chicken is cut in small pieces, the less-expensive thigh meat can be used.*
*It is important to use skinless chicken, which contains far less fat than portions with skin.*
*Any seasonal salad vegetable can be used, although the predominant flavour should be citrus.*

Calories per serving: 180
Points per serving: 3½
Total Points per recipe: 7

*2 small boneless, skinless chicken*
*   thighs*
*1 teaspoon olive oil*
*1 teaspoon dried mixed herbs*
*grated zest and juice of 1 lime or*
*   lemon*
*1 tomato, skinned (see page 109),*
*   de-seeded and chopped*
*½ red chilli, de-seeded and sliced*
*   very thinly*
*4 new potatoes, cooked in their skins*
*   and cubed*
*4 spring onions, sliced*
*2 tablespoons chopped fresh*
*   coriander*
*salt and freshly ground black pepper*

**1**   Preheat the grill to medium.

**2**   Rub the chicken pieces with oil and season with the mixed herbs and salt and pepper.

**3**   Grill for 15–20 minutes, turning frequently.

**4**   Leave to cool and then cut into bite-sized pieces.

**5**   Transfer to a non-metallic dish or bowl and combine with the remaining ingredients.

**6**   Cover and refrigerate for at least 4 hours, to allow the flavours to develop.

# SALADE NIÇOISE

◆

*Serves 2 ◆ Preparation time 10 minutes ◆ Freezing not recommended*
*I've included the ingredients for a genuine Nice-style salad. If you don't like*
*anchovies or olives, just leave them out. You could, of course, invent your own mixed salad*
*in the style of where you live, using vegetables which grow in your garden or allotment*
*with your favourite ingredients.*

Calories per serving: 150
Points per serving: 2
Total Points per recipe: 4

*60 g (2 oz) french beans, topped*
*and tailed*

*a few Cos lettuce leaves*

*2 tomatoes, quartered*

*100 g can of tuna in water, drained*
*and flaked*

*4 anchovy fillets, drained and*
*chopped*

*1 hard-boiled egg, shelled and*
*quartered*

*10 black olives*

*1 tablespoon low-fat vinaigrette*
*dressing*

*salt and freshly ground black pepper*

**1**   Plunge the beans into boiling water. Leave for 5 minutes, and then rinse in cold water and drain well.

**2**   Tear the salad leaves and place them in a bowl. Add the tomatoes, tuna, anchovies, egg, olives and drained beans.

**3**   Toss together gently with a little seasoning, and spoon the dressing over just before serving.

*Kitchen Notes*
Blanching is done for a variety of
reasons; to remove the skins of tomatoes
and almonds; to remove the bitter juices
of orange and lemon zest; and to
preserve the colour of vegetables before
freezing. The food is covered with boiling
water for 1 minute or more, immediately
plunged into cold water to prevent
further cooking, and then drained.

◆

# RATATOUILLE CRUMBLE

♦

*Serves 6 ♦ Preparation time 35 minutes ♦ Cooking time 1 hour ♦ Freezing recommended*
*Mediterranean vegetables are grown all year round under glass in Holland, but have the most*
*superb flavour when they are in season, having ripened in the Mediterranean sunshine.*

Calories per serving: 90
Points per serving: ½
Total Points per recipe: 3

1 aubergine, sliced

1 tablespoon olive oil

1 onion, chopped

2 garlic cloves, sliced

1 green pepper, de-seeded and cut
 in strips

1 red pepper, de-seeded and cut
 in strips

4 courgettes, sliced

6 plum tomatoes, skinned (see page
 109), de-seeded and halved

6 tablespoons fresh wholemeal
 breadcrumbs (see page 135)

salt and freshly ground black pepper

**1**  Preheat the oven to Gas Mark 4/180°C/350°F.

**2**  Liberally salt the aubergine slices and place them in a colander
with a plate on top to weight them down. Allow to drain over a sink for
30 minutes. Then rinse thoroughly and pat dry with kitchen paper,
squeezing out as much water as possible.

**3**  Meanwhile, heat the olive oil in a flameproof casserole, and gently
cook the onion and garlic for 5 minutes.

**4**  Add all the prepared vegetables to the casserole and stir well to blend.

**5**  Season well, cover and simmer for 30 minutes.

**6**  Remove the lid and sprinkle the breadcrumbs evenly over
the ratatouille.

**7**  Bake for 30 minutes more.

# SPAGHETTI WITH SUMMER VEGETABLES

*Serves 4 ♦ Preparation time 10 minutes ♦ Cooking time 15 minutes ♦ Freezing recommended*
*Pasta cooks so quickly that you can put together a tasty and nutritious meal in mere*
*minutes. Spaghetti is usually made with water and flour only and so is less rich*
*and has fewer Calories than egg pasta.*

Calories per serving: 415
Points per serving: 5
Total Points per recipe: 20

360 g (12 oz) spaghetti

1 tablespoon vegetable oil

1 onion, chopped

1 garlic clove, crushed

240 g (8 oz) mangetout, topped
   and tailed

240 g (8 oz) tomatoes, skinned (see
   page 109) and chopped

2 courgettes, sliced thinly

1 yellow pepper, de-seeded and
   chopped

1 tablespoon chopped fresh
   marjoram

salt and freshly ground black pepper

60 g (2 oz) half-fat parmesan
   cheese, grated, to serve

**1** Cook the pasta in a large pan of lightly salted boiling water for 10–12 minutes, or according to the packet instructions. Drain well.

**2** Meanwhile, heat the oil in a smaller pan and cook the onion and garlic until soft but not browned.

**3** Add the mangetout, tomatoes, courgettes and pepper to the pan. Cook for 5 minutes and then stir in the marjoram. Season to taste.

**4** Serve the spaghetti with the sauce piled on top in one large bowl or as individual servings. Hand round the grated cheese separately.

*Kitchen Notes*
You may read in some books that cooked pasta should be rinsed with cold water to stop the cooking process. However, for a hot dish, the sticky surface of the pasta needs to be retained so that the sauce will adhere, so do not rinse. Pasta needs rinsing *only* if it is to be used for salads, so that it does not congeal.

♦

GAZPACHO SOUP *(page 126)*
SPAGHETTI WITH SUMMER VEGETABLES

# SPICED BEEF PATTIES

♦

*Serves 4 ♦ Preparation time 10 minutes ♦ Cooking time 20 minutes ♦ Freezing recommended*
*These patties might be called seekh kebabs on an Indian menu. There are lots of ingredients,*
*but the melding of their flavours creates an unforgettable taste. You can prepare the*
*patties ahead and refrigerate them until ready to cook. Serve them with pitta or naan bread*
*and some Raita (see page 201).*

Calories per serving: 195
Points per serving: 3
Total Points per recipe: 12

*1 tablespoon vegetable oil*

*1 onion, grated*

*1 garlic clove, crushed*

*2.5 cm (1-inch) piece of fresh root*
  *ginger, grated or chopped finely*

*1 teaspoon ground cumin*

*1 teaspoon ground coriander*

*240 g (8 oz) finely ground minced*
  *beef or lamb (see page 63)*

*1 egg, beaten*

*3 tablespoons fresh breadcrumbs*
  *(see page 135)*

*1 tablespoon chopped fresh mint*

*juice of 1 lemon*

*½ teaspoon chilli powder*

*salt and freshly ground black pepper*

**1**  Heat the oil in a small pan and add the onion, garlic, ginger, cumin and coriander. Cook for 5 minutes and then allow to cool.

**2**  Mix together the mince, egg, breadcrumbs, mint, lemon juice and chilli powder.

**3**  Stir in the onion mixture and some seasoning and blend together well.

**4**  Using wetted hands, shape the mixture into patties about 5 cm (2 inches) in diameter and 1 cm (½ inch) thick. Preheat the grill or barbecue.

**5**  Grill or barbecue for 5 minutes on each side.

# PAN BAGNAT

◆

*Serves 2 ◆ Preparation time 10 minutes ◆ Cooking time 20 minutes ◆ Freezing not recommended*
*This variation on the sandwich theme originates in the Mediterranean.*

Calories per serving: 390
Points per serving: 5½
Total Points per recipe: 11

2 red peppers

1 baguette, split in half lengthways

2 plum tomatoes, sliced

1 red onion, sliced thinly

6 stoned black olives

1 tablespoon low-fat vinaigrette
   dressing

1 garlic clove, crushed

6 fresh basil leaves

salt and freshly ground black pepper

**1**   Skin the peppers (see below). Slice in strips.

**2**   Scoop out a little of the bread from the bottom half of the loaf.

**3**   Spread the peppers, tomatoes, onion and olives in the hollow, seasoning and pressing down well between each addition.

**4**   Mix the dressing with the crushed garlic and drizzle it over the vegetables. Arrange the basil leaves on top. Replace the top half of the bread.

**5**   Roll the bread in a barely damp tea towel and weight it down with something heavy until ready to serve. If you're taking it on a picnic, wrap in kitchen foil rather than a tea towel.

**6**   Cut the loaf in slices and provide plenty of napkins as the filling will be quite moist.

**VARIATION:** You could add chopped anchovy fillets or cured sausage. This will make it unsuitable for vegetarians. Remember to add any extra Points.

*Kitchen Notes*
To skin peppers, grill whole peppers
under a medium grill for 20 minutes,
turning occasionally. They will turn
quite black before they are done. Put
them in a polythene bag, tie the top
and leave to cool. Remove the skins
under running water, and then cut the
pepper in half and discard the seeds.
Save any juices for your dish.
◆

# PILAFF WITH PEAS

◆

*Serves 4 ◆ Preparation time 10 minutes ◆ Cooking time 30 minutes ◆ Freezing recommended*
*Use fresh peas for this Indian-spiced rice dish. You can use whatever strength curry powder you*
*prefer. This pilaff can be served with any dish instead of plain boiled rice.*

Calories per serving: 430
Points per serving: 6
Total Points per recipe: 24

*1 tablespoon vegetable oil*

*1 onion, chopped*

*2 garlic cloves, crushed*

*2 teaspoons curry powder*

*1 teaspoon ground cinnamon*

*360 g (12 oz) long-grain rice*

*300 ml (½ pint) vegetable stock*

*240 g (8 oz) shelled peas*

*salt and freshly ground black pepper*

*fresh coriander leaves, to garnish*

*(optional)*

**1**  Heat the oil in a large pan and cook the onion, garlic, and curry powder for 3 minutes.

**2**  Add the cinnamon and rice and stir to mix.

**3**  Pour in the stock and bring to the boil. Reduce to a simmer and cover.

**4**  Simmer for 15 minutes, checking occasionally in case more stock is needed.

**5**  Add the peas and cook for 10 more minutes, stirring occasionally.

**6**  Season to taste and transfer to a bowl or platter. Garnish with coriander leaves.

# STUFFED MARROW

◆

*Serves 6 ◆ Preparation time 10 minutes ◆ Cooking time 1 hour ◆ Freezing recommended*
*If using minced lamb, try to use fresh rosemary, as the flavours marry beautifully.*

Calories per serving: 175
Points per serving: 3
Total Points per recipe: 18

*1 marrow, about 1 kg (2 lb)*

*360 g (12 oz) minced beef or lamb*
*(see page 63)*

*6 tablespoons fresh wholemeal*
*breadcrumbs (see below)*

*1 onion, chopped finely*

*1 tablespoon chopped fresh parsley*
*or rosemary*

*2 tablespoons tomato purée*

*1 egg, beaten*

*salt and freshly ground black pepper*

**1**  Preheat the oven to Gas Mark 4/180°C/350°F.

**2**  Peel the marrow, cut in half lengthways and scoop out the seeds.

**3**  Mix the remaining ingredients together and spoon into one half of the marrow.

**4**  Use the other half as a lid, and place the marrow in an ovenproof dish. Cover with greaseproof paper or kitchen foil.

**5**  Bake for 1 hour, and then serve sliced on a platter.

**COOK'S NOTE:** A well-flavoured tomato sauce is the best accompaniment for stuffed marrow. For a super-quick, no-Points sauce, mix together 1 finely chopped onion, 1 crushed garlic clove, 300 ml (½ pint) passata, 1 teaspoon dried mixed herbs and some seasoning. Heat, stirring occasionally, for 5 minutes.

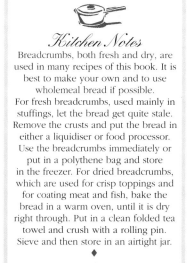

### Kitchen Notes

Breadcrumbs, both fresh and dry, are used in many recipes of this book. It is best to make your own and to use wholemeal bread if possible. For fresh breadcrumbs, used mainly in stuffings, let the bread get quite stale. Remove the crusts and put the bread in either a liquidiser or food processor. Use the breadcrumbs immediately or put in a polythene bag and store in the freezer. For dried breadcrumbs, which are used for crisp toppings and for coating meat and fish, bake the bread in a warm oven, until it is dry right through. Put in a clean folded tea towel and crush with a rolling pin. Sieve and then store in an airtight jar.

◆

# SUMMER PUDDING

◆

*Serves 4 ◆ Preparation time 10 minutes + overnight soaking ◆ Freezing not recommended*
*Any mix of soft fruits can be used for this dish, but they must be ripe and I do*
*recommend strawberries and raspberries. Serve with Weight Watchers vanilla ice cream*
*or some very-low-fat fromage frais.*

Calories per serving: 170
Points per serving: 2
Total Points per recipe: 8

*480 g (1 lb) mixed soft fruit*
  *(e.g. strawberries, raspberries,*
  *red and blackcurrants, pitted*
  *cherries and blackberries)*
*artificial sweetener, to taste*
*6–8 slices of white bread, crusts*
  *removed*
*fresh mint leaves, to garnish*
  *(optional)*

**1**  Put the fruit and 2 tablespoons of water in a pan and heat gently for 5 minutes, until the juices start to run but the berries retain their texture.

**2**  Add artificial sweetener to taste.

**3**  Line the base and sides of a 900 ml (1¾-pint) pudding basin with the bread.

**4**  Spoon in the fruit and juice, and then cover with more bread and place a saucer or small plate on top.

**5**  Weight the basin down with something heavy, such as a can of fruit.

**6**  Leave somewhere cool overnight.

**7**  Remove the weight and plate and loosen the sides of the pudding. Invert on to a serving plate and decorate with fresh mint leaves, if you like.

# PEACH AND RASPBERRY CRISP

◆

*Serves 4 ◆ Preparation time 10 minutes ◆ Cooking time 30 minutes ◆ Freezing recommended*
*This is a variation of that perennial family favourite – apple crumble. Serve it with low-fat*
*natural yogurt or Weight Watchers vanilla ice cream.*

Calories per serving: 205
Points per serving: 3½
Total Points per recipe: 14

4 peaches, skinned with stones
  removed (use method for skinning
  tomatoes on page 109)
120 g (4 oz) raspberries
2 tablespoons orange juice
60 g (2 oz) plain flour
3 tablespoons granular artificial
  sweetener
5 tablespoons rolled oats (porridge
  oats)
1 teaspoon ground cinnamon
60 g (2 oz) low-fat spread

**1** Preheat the oven to Gas Mark 5/190°C/375°F.

**2** Slice the peaches into a small ovenproof dish.

**3** Spoon over the raspberries and orange juice.

**4** Mix together the flour, sweetener, rolled oats and cinnamon. Using a fork, blend in the low-fat spread.

**5** Spoon the crumble mixture over the fruit and bake for 30 minutes or until golden brown.

**VARIATION:** Substitute nectarines for the peaches, or blueberries or blackberries for the raspberries.

*Autumn*

•

# MENU PLAN

## MONDAY

**BREAKFAST**
½ grapefruit with granular artificial sweetener:
½ Point
1 slice toast: 1 Point
1 teaspoon low-fat spread:
½ Point
1 heaped teaspoon jam:
½ Point

♦

**LUNCH**
*Chicken, Bean and Pepper Stir-fry (page 147):*
2½ Points
1 medium portion cooked rice: 3 Points
salad of tomatoes, red onion and parsley with fat-free salad dressing:
0 Points

♦

**DINNER**
1 medium loin pork chop, grilled: 5 Points
2 scoops mashed potato:
2 Points
swede and carrots:
0 Points
gravy made with
1 teaspoon gravy granules:
½ Point
1 small can (210 g/7 oz) fruit cocktail in natural juice: 1 Point
1 tablespoon whipping cream: 1½ Points

————

**MILK**
300 ml (½ pint) skimmed milk: 1 Point

**TREAT**
3 boiled sweets: 1 Point

## TUESDAY

**BREAKFAST**
1 small can (210 g/7 oz) mandarin segments in natural juice: 1 Point
1 small tub low-fat natural yogurt: 1½ Points
1 slice toast: 1 Point
1 teaspoon low-fat spread:
½ Point

♦

**LUNCH**
*Baked Potato with Blue Cheese and Pear (page 161):* 7 Points
salad of lettuce and tomato with fat-free salad dressing: 0 Points
3 plums: ½ Point

♦

**DINNER**
Weight Watchers from Heinz Frozen Ocean Pie:
4½ Points
2 tablespoons peas:
1 Point
leeks and carrots:
0 Points
1 medium portion apples stewed with sugar:
1 Point

————

**MILK**
300 ml (½ pint) skimmed milk: 1 Point

**TREAT**
1 mug drinking chocolate:
1 Point

## WEDNESDAY

**BREAKFAST**
2 slices bread: 2 Points
2 teaspoons low-fat spread:
1 Point
2 heaped teaspoons jam or marmalade: 1 Point

♦

**LUNCH**
*Hearty Potato and Paprika Soup (page 178):* 2 Points
1 medium crusty roll:
2 Points
1 pear: 1 Point

♦

**DINNER**
2 medium slices honey-roast ham: 2 Points
1 large boiled egg: 2 Points
1 medium portion boiled potatoes: 2 Points
1 large portion sweetcorn:
½ Point
cauliflower: 0 Points
*Stewed Cranberries and Bananas (page 187):*
3 Points

————

**MILK**
300 ml (½ pint) skimmed milk: 1 Point

**TREAT**
1 small pot Weight Watchers from Heinz fat-free fromage frais:
½ Point

## THURSDAY

BREAKFAST
1 medium bowl porridge
made with 150 ml
(1/4 pint) skimmed milk
and granular artificial
sweetener: 2 Points
1 small glass fruit juice:
1/2 Point
♦
LUNCH
1 small beefburger:
3 Points
1 slice low-fat cheese:
1 Point
1 medium beefburger bun:
2 Points
onion and tomato garnish:
0 Points
1 orange or apple:
1/2 Point
♦
DINNER
*Trout with Herb Stuffing*
*(page 169):* 3 1/2 Points
1 medium portion boiled
potato: 2 Points
2 tablespoons peas:
1 Point
carrots and courgettes:
0 Points
6 plums: 1 Point

———

MILK
450 ml (3/4 pint) skimmed
milk: 1 1/2 Points

TREAT
1 small tub low-fat fruit
yogurt: 2 Points

## FRIDAY

BREAKFAST
1 small glass fruit juice:
1/2 Point
grilled tomatoes: 0 Points
1 slice toast: 1 Point
1 teaspoon low-fat spread:
1/2 Point
♦
LUNCH
*Leek and Rice Salad*
*(page 176):* 2 1/2 Points
1 slice granary bread:
1 1/2 Points
1 teaspoon low-fat spread:
1/2 Point
tomato salad: 0 Points
1 small bunch grapes:
1 Point
♦
DINNER
*Chicken and Pepper*
*Stir-Fry (page 184):*
4 Points
1 medium portion cooked
pasta: 2 Points
steamed corgettes:
0 Points
2 tablespoons peas:
1 Point
1 small tub low-fat natural
yogurt: 1 1/2 Points
1 medium portion plums
stewed with sugar:
1 Point

———

MILK
300 ml (1/2 pint) skimmed
milk: 1 Point

TREAT
1 small pot crème
caramel: 2 Points

## SATURDAY

BREAKFAST
1/2 grapefruit with granular
artificial sweetener:
1/2 Point
1 small tub low-fat natural
yogurt: 1 1/2 Points
♦
LUNCH
*Omelette Sandwich*
*(page 147):* 5 1/2 Points
1 slice *Banana Bread*
*(page 171):* 3 Points
1 pear: 1 Point
♦
DINNER
stir-fry made with peppers,
bean sprouts, onion,
broccoli and cauliflower
florets, french beans,
mangetout, mushrooms
and water chestnuts,
1 medium portion prawns
and low-fat cooking spray:
1 Point
105 g (3 1/2 oz)
blackberries and
1 medium cooking apple
stewed in 1 teaspoon
sugar: 2 Points
1 1/2 tablespoons single
cream: 1 1/2 Points

———

MILK
300 ml (1/2 pint) skimmed
milk: 1 Point

TREAT
1 medium slice
Battenburg cake: 3 Points

## SUNDAY

BREAKFAST
1 small glass fruit juice:
1/2 Point
1 slice toast: 1 Point
1 teaspoon low-fat spread:
1/2 Point
3 tablespoons baked
beans: 1 Point
♦
LUNCH
1/2 medium Galia melon:
1 Point
1 can Weight Watchers
from Heinz Italiana
Vegetable Ravioli in
Tomato Sauce: 4 Points
green salad with fat-free
salad dressing: 0 Points
♦
DINNER
*Duck with Pancakes and*
*Plum Sauce (page 164):*
9 Points
1 small can (210 g/7 oz)
apricots in natural juice:
1 Point
1 small glass wine:
1 Point

———

MILK
150 ml (1/4 pint) skimmed
milk: 1/2 Point

TREAT
1 tube Weight Watchers
Fruities: 1/2 Point

# September

Foods with an autumnal flavour start to appear this month. Stoned fruits such as plums, greengages and damsons should be plentiful. More varieties of English dessert and cooking apples are available, and pears are beginning to arrive on the shelves. Blackberries are ripe now and make an enjoyable excuse for getting out into the country to pick some. They are high in fibre and are delicious eaten on their own or mixed with sliced apples and a dollop of yogurt. Wild mushrooms are also available this month, and their earthy flavour makes a nice change from field mushrooms.

Marrows make their first appearance of the season, and courgettes get larger. There should also be plenty of squash and pumpkins about, and any of these vegetables are ideal for stuffing with vegetable and meat fillings.

VENISON WITH CHESNUTS *(page 153)*
STUFFED SQUASH *(page 146)*
BAKED PLUMS *(page 155)*

# MUSHROOMS ON TOAST

◆

*Serves 1 ◆ Preparation time 5 minutes ◆ Cooking time 5 minutes ◆ Freezing not recommended*
*Mushrooms on toast are just right for a crisp September morning. You could serve these*
*with a few bacon rashers or a grilled tomato, for a heartier weekend brunch.*
*There are many varieties of mushroom in the shops now, from the ordinary flat and*
*button mushrooms to the 'meaty' chestnut (brown-skinned) ones and the more exotic*
*oyster mushrooms. Choose any variety for this dish.*

Calories per serving: 115
Points per serving: 1

*120 g (4 oz) mushrooms, sliced*
*2 tablespoons milk*
*1 tablespoon chopped fresh parsley*
*1 slice of wholemeal bread*
*salt and freshly ground black pepper*

**1**  Put the mushrooms in a pan, with the milk and seasoning.

**2**  Heat for 5 minutes, until the mushrooms are softened, and then stir in the parsley.

**3**  Toast the bread on both sides.

**4**  Drain any excess liquid from the mushrooms and reserve for use in a soup or gravy, if you like.

**5**  Serve the mushrooms on the toast.

# AUBERGINE SLICES WITH MINTED YOGURT

◆

*Serves 2 ◆ Preparation time 5 minutes + 30 minutes salting ◆ Cooking time 10 minutes ◆*
*Freezing recommended*
*Do use olive oil in this recipe: one flavoured with basil or garlic would be even better, to make the*
*flavour of this dish Mediterranean all the way.*

Calories per serving: 180
Points per serving: 3½
Total Points per recipe: 7

*1 aubergine, cut in 1 cm (½-inch)*
  *thick slices*
*2 tablespoons olive oil*
*150 g tub of low-fat natural yogurt*
*1 tablespoon chopped fresh mint*
*salt and freshly ground black pepper*

**1**  Liberally salt the aubergine slices, placing them in a colander with a plate on top to weight them down. Allow to drain over the sink for 30 minutes.

**2**  Rinse them well, to remove all the salt, and pat each slice dry, squeezing slightly to remove as much liquid as possible.

**3**  Preheat the grill or barbecue.

**4**  Spread the aubergine slices on a work surface and brush both sides with olive oil. Season with pepper only.

**5**  Grill for 5 minutes on each side.

**6**  Meanwhile, mix the yogurt with the mint.

**7**  Arrange the aubergine slices on a serving plate and drizzle the yogurt over them.

**WEIGHT WATCHERS TIP:** Salting aubergines not only allows any bitter juices to drain away, but it makes it more difficult for the aubergine to absorb oil. This is particularly important when you are frying aubergine.

# TUNA, TOMATO AND WATERCRESS SALAD

◆

*Serves 4 ◆ Preparation time 5 minutes ◆ Freezing not recommended*
*Many types of tomatoes are in season now, and you may like to choose a variety*
*according to how you want to serve your salad.*

Calories per serving: 80
Points per serving: 1
Total Points per recipe: 4

*240 g (8 oz) tomatoes*
*1 packet of watercress*
*juice of 1 lemon*
*1 red-skinned apple, cored,*
  *quartered and sliced thinly*
*1 Little Gem lettuce*

**FOR THE DRESSING:**
*100 g can of tuna in water, drained*
  *and flaked*
*150 g tub of low-fat natural yogurt*
*1 teaspoon chopped fresh parsley*

**1**  Prepare the tomatoes: large tomatoes can be sliced, round or plum tomatoes quartered, and cherry tomatoes can be left whole. Put the tomatoes and watercress in a serving bowl or plate, or in individual bowls.

**2**  Drizzle half the lemon juice over the apple slices and add the slices to the salad.

**3**  Add the lettuce leaves to the salad.

**4**  Make the dressing by mashing the tuna with the yogurt and the remaining lemon juice. Stir in the parsley.

**5**  Pour the dressing over the salad just before serving, and toss well.

# HAM, PLUM AND FENNEL SALAD

◆

*Serves 1 ◆ Preparation time 10 minutes ◆ Freezing not recommended*
*Ham goes well with fruit, and this salad is suitable for a light meal or as a starter.*

Calories per serving: 90
Points per serving: 2

*60 g (2 oz) thinly sliced ham*
*2–3 plums or greengages, halved,*
  *with stones removed*
*1 tablespoon orange juice*
*½ fennel bulb, with frondy leaves*
*1 tablespoon fat-free salad dressing*
*freshly ground black pepper*

**1**  Arrange the ham on one side of a plate.

**2**  Slice the plums and dip them in orange juice to prevent them from browning.

**3**  Cut the leaves from the fennel and chop roughly. Slice the fennel bulb thinly.

**4**  Toss the plums and fennel with the salad dressing and season with black pepper.

**5**  Arrange the salad on the empty side of the salad plate.

HAM, PLUM AND FENNEL SALAD
TUNA, TOMATO AND WATERCRESS SALAD

# STUFFED SQUASH OR PUMPKIN

◆

*Serves 4 ◆ Preparation time 10 minutes ◆ Cooking time 45 minutes ◆ Freezing not recommended*
*This stuffing could be used with other vegetables, such as peppers, tomatoes, onions or marrow.*

Calories per serving: 260
Points per serving: 2½
Total Points per recipe: 10

Ⓥ

1 small pumpkin or acorn squash,
    halved lengthways and de-seeded
1 tablespoon vegetable oil
1 onion, chopped
1 garlic clove, crushed
120 g (4 oz) mushrooms, chopped
120 g (4 oz) long-grain rice
1 teaspoon ground cinnamon
150 ml (¼ pint) vegetable stock
120 g (4 oz) seedless green grapes
salt and freshly ground black pepper

**1**  Place the pumpkin or squash cut-side down on a baking sheet and bake in a preheated oven at Gas Mark 4/180°C/350°F for about 45 minutes.

**2**  Prepare the stuffing while the pumpkin is cooking. Heat the oil in a pan and cook the onion and garlic until soft but not browned.

**3**  Stir in the mushrooms, rice and cinnamon. Add the stock and simmer for 15 minutes, adding more water if necessary.

**4**  Halve the grapes and add them to the stuffing. Season to taste.

**5**  Spoon the stuffing into the cooked pumpkin and serve at once, cut in quarters.

**VARIATIONS:** Raisins or sultanas can be substituted for the grapes. Add with the mushrooms and rice. Points per serving will be 3½.

# SCALLOP AND TARRAGON PIE

◆

*Serves 4 ◆ Preparation time 10 minutes ◆ Cooking time 30 minutes ◆ Freezing recommended*

Calories per serving: 215
Points per serving: 3
Total Points per recipe: 12

720 g (1½ lb) potatoes
300 ml (½ pint) skimmed milk
1 tablespoon cornflour
240 g (8 oz) small scallops
240 g (8 oz) button or field
    mushrooms, sliced
1 onion, chopped
1 tablespoon tomato purée
1 tablespoon chopped fresh tarragon
salt and freshly ground black pepper

**1**  Peel and halve the potatoes. Boil for 20 minutes, or until cooked through.

**2**  Meanwhile, blend 150 ml (¼ pint) of the milk with the cornflour and bring to the boil. If it's too thick, slacken with a little cold water.

**3**  Add the scallops, mushrooms, onion, tomato purée and tarragon, and season to taste. Preheat the grill to medium.

**4**  Put the fish mixture in an ovenproof dish or individual freezer dishes.

**5**  Drain the potatoes, reserving a little of the cooking liquid.

**6**  Mash the potatoes with the remaining skimmed milk, to make a soft topping; add a little potato liquid, if necessary.

**7**  Spoon the potato over the fish and rough the surface up using a fork. Grill until golden brown on top.

# OMELETTE SANDWICH

*Serves 2 ◆ Preparation time 5 minutes ◆ Cooking time 5 minutes ◆ Freezing not recommended*

Calories per serving: 375
Points per serving: 5½
Total Points per recipe: 11

60 g (2 oz) button mushrooms
1 tablespoon vegetable oil
2 tomatoes, skinned (see page 109),
    de-seeded and chopped
2 eggs, beaten
1 tablespoon chopped fresh chives
2 wholemeal pitta breads
salt and freshly ground black pepper
mixed salad leaves, to serve

1   Slice the mushrooms. Heat the oil in an omelette pan and sauté the mushrooms and tomatoes for 3 minutes.

2   Beat together the eggs, 2 tablespoons of water and the chives, along with some seasoning.

3   Pour the eggs into the pan and cook, drawing the cooked edges into the middle of the pan and allowing the liquid to run away from the centre.

4   When cooked on one side, flip the omelette over and cook the other side, or put it under a preheated grill until set.

5   Warm the pittas under the grill or in the microwave.

6   Cut the omelette into quarters and the pittas in half and put one quarter in each pitta 'pocket'.

7   Serve on plates with the salad leaves. A little low-fat salad dressing can be used to coat the leaves, if you like.

# CHICKEN, BEAN AND PEPPER STIR-FRY

*Serves 4 ◆ Preparation time 10 minutes ◆ Cooking time 15 minutes*
*Freezing not recommended*

Calories per serving: 195
Points per serving: 2½
Total Points per recipe: 10

1 red onion
360 g (12 oz) runner beans
1 red pepper
240 g (8 oz) Tandoori or Chinese
    flavoured ready-cooked chicken
1 tablespoon vegetable oil
2.5 cm (1-inch) piece of fresh root
    ginger, peeled and chopped
1 tablespoon sesame seeds
1 tablespoon soy sauce
1 teaspoon sesame oil

1   First prepare the vegetables and chicken. Halve the red onion lengthways and slice. Top and tail the runner beans; slice thinly. Halve and de-seed the red pepper; cut into slices. Cut the chicken into thin slices.

2   Heat the vegetable oil in a wok and stir-fry the ginger, sesame seeds and onion for 5 minutes.

3   Add the beans and pepper and stir-fry for 5 more minutes.

4   Add the chicken and heat through. Stir in the soy sauce and sesame oil and serve at once.

# CHICKEN AND CELERY RICE

◆

*Serves 4 ◆ Preparation time 10 minutes ◆ Cooking time 40 minutes ◆ Freezing recommended*
*Brown rice has a higher proportion of fibre than white rice and, although it does take longer to*
*cook, it has a delicious nutty flavour. Try using boil-in-the-bag rice, which can be prepared in*
*the microwave as well as on the hob.*

Calories per serving: 370
Points per serving: 5
Total Points per recipe: 20

*240 g (8 oz) brown rice, cooked*
*according to the packet*
*instructions*
*2 boneless, skinless chicken breasts*
*150 ml (¼ pint) unsweetened*
*apple juice*
*1 red-skinned apple, cored and*
*sliced*
*1 tablespoon lemon juice*
*1 head of celery, cut in 2.5 cm*
*(1-inch) slices, with leaves*
*reserved*
*60 g (2 oz) raisins*
*1 tablespoon wholegrain mustard*
*salt and freshly ground black pepper*

**1**  Drain the cooked rice and keep warm.

**2**  Season the chicken breasts and poach in the apple juice for 20 minutes.

**3**  Remove from the pan and cut into bite-sized pieces, reserving the poaching liquid.

**4**  Toss the apple slices in lemon juice, to prevent them from browning.

**5**  Heat the rice and chicken together and stir in the apple, celery, raisins and mustard. Season to taste and add enough hot poaching liquid to keep the dish moist.

**6**  Garnish with the celery leaves and serve hot.

SCALLOP AND TARRAGON PIE *(page 146)*

# SAVOURY PANCAKES

◆

*Serves 4* ◆ *Preparation time 15 minutes* ◆ *Cooking time 20 minutes* ◆
*Freezing recommended before stuffing the pancakes*
*The basic pancake mixture will make pancakes for either a savoury or a sweet filling.*
*They freeze beautifully – interleave the cooked pancakes with freezer film and then you can take*
*as many or as few from the freezer as you need. This filling is Greek in flavour, but other ideas*
*are to be found at the end of the recipe.*

Calories per serving: 285
Points per serving: 5½
Total Points per recipe: 22

**FOR THE PANCAKES:**

*120 g (4 oz) plain flour*

*1 egg*

*300 ml (½ pint) skimmed milk*

*a little oil for brushing the pan*

**FOR THE FILLING:**

*1 green pepper, de-seeded and*
*chopped*

*1 red pepper, de-seeded and*
*chopped*

*2 large tomatoes, chopped*

*120 g (4 oz) stoned black olives,*
*chopped*

*120 g (4 oz) feta cheese, cut in*
*small cubes*

*1 tablespoon chopped fresh parsley*

*salt and freshly ground black pepper*

**1**  Sieve the flour into a bowl and make a well in the centre.

**2**  Break the egg in and gradually combine with the flour.

**3**  Gradually add the milk and beat into the flour.

**4**  Beat together all the ingredients until smooth (or use a liquidiser or food processor).

**5**  Brush a non-stick or well seasoned pan with a little oil and heat.

**6**  Pour in a little batter and swirl round the pan to coat the base. When small bubbles appear on the surface and it is brown on the underside, flip the pancake over to cook the other side.

**7**  Fold the pancake into quarters and transfer to a warm plate. Make seven more pancakes.

**8**  Mix together all the filling ingredients and spoon into the pancakes. Serve immediately.

**VARIATIONS:** Use mushroom and ham, bolognese sauce, chicken and celery, or prawn and broccoli.

Instead of folding the pancakes into cornets, you could leave them flat and roll them with the filling inside.

# COURGETTE RISOTTO

◆

*Serves 2 ◆ Preparation time 10 minutes ◆ Cooking time 20 minutes ◆ Freezing recommended*
*Risottos have a delicious creamy texture and flavour. They do require a bit of attention when*
*they are cooking, but the final result is well worth the effort. Squash or pumpkin*
*can be substituted for the courgettes.*

Calories per serving: 345
Points per serving: 5
Total Points per recipe: 10

*1 tablespoon vegetable oil*

*1 onion, chopped*

*1 garlic clove, crushed*

*4 courgettes, sliced*

*120 g (4 oz) risotto rice*

*1 tablespoon lemon juice*

*210 ml (7 fl oz) hot vegetable stock*

*1 tablespoon chopped fresh parsley*

*salt and freshly ground black pepper*

**1**   Heat the oil in a pan and slowly cook the onion and garlic until soft but not browned.

**2**   Add the courgettes and rice and stir well.

**3**   Add the lemon juice and a few spoonfuls of stock. Stir until the rice has absorbed the liquid.

**4**   Continue to add the stock in small batches, stirring constantly, until the liquid is absorbed.

**5**   When the rice is creamy but still has a little 'bite', add the parsley and seasoning and serve immediately.

# LIVER AND BROCCOLI STIR-FRY IN TORTILLAS

◆

*Serves 2 ◆ Preparation time 10 minutes ◆ Cooking time 10 minutes ◆ Freezing not recommended*
*This stir-fry has been influenced by Tex-Mex cuisine and is served in tortillas, with a spicy tomato*
*sauce poured over the top. Liver is rich in vitamins and minerals, but if you dislike it,*
*use thinly sliced lamb fillet instead.*

Calories per serving: 550
Points per serving: 8
Total Points per recipe: 16

*180 g (6 oz) lamb's or calf's liver or*
*lamb fillet, cut in thin strips*

*1 tablespoon plain flour, seasoned*

*1 tablespoon vegetable oil*

*1 garlic clove, sliced thinly*

*2.5 cm (1-inch) piece of fresh root*
*ginger, chopped finely*

*½ red pepper, de-seeded and sliced*
*thinly*

*1 small head of broccoli, split into*
*tiny florets*

*2 teaspoons soy sauce*

**TO SERVE:**

*salt and freshly ground black pepper*

*4 tortillas*

*Tomato Salsa (page 118)*

**1**  Toss the meat in the seasoned flour and discard any unused flour.

**2**  Heat the oil in a wok or frying-pan and stir-fry the garlic and ginger for 1 minute.

**3**  Add the liver or fillet and stir-fry for 3 minutes.

**4**  Add the red pepper and broccoli and cook for 3 more minutes.

**5**  Stir in the soy sauce and season to taste.

**6**  Divide the stir-fry between the 4 tortillas and roll them up. Place in a warmed serving dish and keep warm.

**7**  Make up the salsa recipe and spoon over the tortillas.

# VENISON WITH CHESTNUTS

♦

*Serves 4 ♦ Preparation time 15 minutes ♦ Cooking time 1¼ hours ♦ Freezing recommended*
*Don't be frightened of venison. It's an ideal meat as it has so little fat. It's similar in flavour to beef,*
*which can be used instead, if you wish. This casserole has an autumnal flavour and can be made*
*with other game meats when they are in season. Serve with baked potatoes, which can be cooked*
*in the top of the oven at the same time (though they may need to start cooking a bit earlier).*

Calories per serving: 345
Points per serving: 5
Total Points per recipe: 20

*480 g (1 lb) stewing venison, cut in*
*bite-sized cubes*

*1 tablespoon plain flour, seasoned*

*1 tablespoon vegetable oil*

*1 onion, chopped*

*4 garlic cloves, peeled*

*600 ml (1 pint) beef stock*

*120 ml (4 fl oz) red wine (optional)*

*4 carrots*

*240 g (8 oz) red cabbage, shredded*

*1 cooking apple, peeled, cored and*
*quartered*

*1 tablespoon chopped fresh thyme or*
*1 teaspoon dried*

*2 bay leaves*

*1 teaspoon ground allspice*

*60 g (2 oz) peeled chestnuts*

*1 tablespoon chopped fresh parsley*

*salt and freshly ground black pepper*

**1**  Preheat the oven to Gas Mark 3/170°C/325°F.

**2**  Toss the venison in seasoned flour.

**3**  Heat the oil in a pan or flameproof casserole and cook the onion and
garlic until golden brown.

**4**  Add the floured meat and sauté, turning occasionally, until sealed on
all sides.

**5**  Add the remaining ingredients, except for the chestnuts and parsley,
and bring to the boil. If using a flameproof casserole, cover and put in the
oven. If using a pan, transfer to a casserole, cover and put in the oven.

**6**  Cook for 1¼ hours, adding the chestnuts 15 minutes before the end of
cooking.

**7**  Season to taste and sprinkle with parsley just before serving.

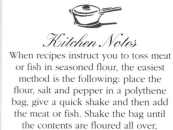

*Kitchen Notes*

When recipes instruct you to toss meat
or fish in seasoned flour, the easiest
method is the following: place the
flour, salt and pepper in a polythene
bag, give a quick shake and then add
the meat or fish. Shake the bag until
the contents are floured all over,
remove from the bag and discard
any excess flour.

♦

# APPLE CRISP

◆

*Serves 2 ◆ Preparation time 10 minutes ◆ Cooking time 10 minutes ◆*
*Freezing recommended for the apple purée only*
*The first English apples are coming in to the shops this month. Choose cooking apples*
*like Bramleys, which will collapse on cooking. The purée can be made in bulk and*
*frozen in small quantities for use later in the year.*
*This is particularly useful if you have an apple tree or if you can pick windfalls.*

Calories per serving: 80
Points per serving: 1½
Total Points per recipe: 3
Ⓥ

*240 g (8 oz) cooking apples, peeled,*
*cored and quartered*
*2 cloves*
*artificial sweetener, to taste*
*120 ml (4 fl oz) very-low-fat*
*fromage frais*
*2 tablespoons fresh wholemeal*
*breadcrumbs (page 135)*
*2 teaspoons granular artificial*
*sweetener*

**1**  Put the apples in a covered pan with the cloves and 2 tablespoons of water.

**2**  Bring to the boil and then simmer until the apples have collapsed.

**3**  Remove from the heat and beat until smooth, removing and discarding the cloves.

**4**  Sweeten to taste and, when cool, stir in the fromage frais and bring it to a soft creamy consistency.

**5**  Divide the purée between the two dishes.

**6**  Toast the breadcrumbs under a medium grill until golden brown and crisp. Mix them with the granular sweetener and sprinkle on the top of the purée just before serving.

# BAKED PLUMS AND GREENGAGES

♦

*Serves 2 ♦ Preparation time 5 minutes ♦ Cooking time 10 minutes ♦ Freezing not recommended*
*These two fruits look well together, the dark purple contrasting beautifully with the yellowy green.*
*Baking the two together with some subtle spicing results in a warming autumnal dessert.*
*Serve it with a scoop of Weight Watchers vanilla ice cream.*

Calories per serving: 85
Points per serving: 2
Total Points per recipe: 4
(V)

*3 dark plums, split, with stones removed*
*5 greengages, split, with stones removed*
*16 flaked almonds*
*½ teaspoon ground cinnamon*
*artificial sweetener, to taste*

**1** Preheat the oven to Gas Mark 4/180°C/350°F.

**2** Arrange the fruit, skin side down, in a single layer on an ovenproof plate.

**3** Put a flaked almond in each hollow and lightly sprinkle with cinnamon.

**4** Drizzle 3 tablespoons of water over the plate and cover with foil.

**5** Bake for 20 minutes and then drain off the juices.

**6** Sweeten the juices with artificial sweetener and pour over the fruit. Serve hot.

# October

Many of the fruits and vegetables that came into season last month continue to be plentiful this month. In particular, the shops will be full of pumpkins ready for Hallowe'en. These vegetables look so exotic, it is hard to believe that they are grown in this country. Their bright yellow flesh adds a golden warmth to soups, casseroles and pies. The flesh can be pureéd after cooking and stored in the freezer for later use, perhaps for Thanksgiving Day if you have North American friends or relatives to celebrate with.

Maincrop (old) potatoes for baking are back in season, and, being high in starch and low in fat, they make an ideal base for a simple supper.

Red cabbages and leeks are becoming available, and can be served raw in salads, cooked on their own, or in stir-fries. Remember that red cabbage must always have an acid ingredient like lemon juice, apple or vinegar added when cooking, to prevent it from turning blue.

LENTILS WITH AUTUMN VEGETABLES *(page 167)*
PUMPKIN SOUP *(page 159)*
PEARS WITH BLACKBERRY SAUCE *(page 171)*
BANANA BREAD *(page 171)*

# BREAKFAST BANANA SPLIT

◆

*Serves 1 ◆ Preparation time 5 minutes ◆ Freezing not recommended*
*Nothing could be more simple than this speedy breakfast and you can replace the apple and*
*blackberries with your own favourite seasonal or dried fruit.*

Calories per serving: 350
Points per serving: 4½

Ⓥ

*1 banana*

*30 g (1 oz) puffed wheat cereal*

*150 g tub of low-fat natural yogurt*

*1 red-skinned apple, cored and*
*sliced*

*1 tablespoon blackberries*

**1**   Peel the banana and cut it lengthways and once across, to make four pieces.

**2**   Arrange the banana around the edge of a dish (a banana split dish would be ideal).

**3**   Put the cereal in the middle and spoon the yogurt over. Top with fruit and serve at once.

# PUMPKIN SOUP

◆

*Serves 6 ◆ Preparation time 10 minutes ◆ Cooking time 30 minutes ◆ Freezing recommended*
*This soup has a glorious autumnal flavour and colour. Although pumpkin dominates, it is full of*
*other winter vegetables. You can substitute acorn squash for the pumpkin, if you prefer.*
*Serve with some fresh, crusty bread.*

Calories per serving: 60
Points per serving: ½
Total Points per recipe: 3

*1 tablespoon vegetable oil*

*1 onion, chopped*

*600 g (1½ lb) pumpkin, peeled,*
  *with seeds removed*

*2 carrots, peeled and sliced*

*1 teaspoon ground ginger*

*½ teaspoon chilli powder*

*1.2 litres (2 pints) vegetable stock*

*1 tablespoon tomato purée*

*salt and freshly ground black pepper*

*a few toasted almond flakes, to*
  *garnish (optional)*

**1**   Heat the oil in a large saucepan and gently cook the onion for
5 minutes.

**2**   Add the other vegetables, with the spices, and toss together. Cook
for 5 more minutes.

**3**   Pour in the stock and the tomato purée and bring to the boil.
Cover and simmer for 20 minutes, or until the vegetables are soft.

**4**   Either liquidise or whizz in a food processor or put through a
coarse sieve.

**5**   Season and reheat. Garnish with the toasted almond flakes, if using,
and serve hot.

*Kitchen Notes*
Home-made soups can be very quick
to make. Add puréed canned beans to
thicken soups instead of using
potatoes, and get the added benefit of
extra fibre. A cheat's tip for enriching
soups quickly and with few extra
Calories, is to stir in a spoonful of diet
fromage frais or Quark
just before serving.
◆

# WATERCRESS, CELERY AND RADISH SALAD

*Serves 2 ◆ Preparation time 10 minutes ◆ Freezing not recommended*

Calories per serving: 120
Points per serving: 1¹/₂
Total Points per recipe: 3

1 bunch of watercress

6 radishes, sliced

120 g (4 oz) half-fat cottage cheese
   with herbs

2 celery sticks, trimmed

¹/₄ teaspoon paprika

**FOR THE DRESSING:**

4 tablespoons low-fat vinaigrette
   dressing

1 tablespoon wholegrain mustard

2 teaspoons lemon juice

salt and freshly ground black pepper

**1** Arrange the watercress and radishes on two plates.

**2** Spoon the cottage cheese down the hollow of each celery stick and cut into 5 cm (2-inch) pieces. Arrange down the middle of the plate and sprinkle with the paprika.

**3** Mix together the dressing ingredients and spoon over the salad.

# CHICKPEA AND TUNA SALAD

*Serves 2 ◆ Preparation time 10 minutes ◆ Freezing not recommended*

Calories per serving: 235
Points per serving: 4
Total Points per recipe: 8

100 g can of tuna in water, drained

420 g can of chickpeas, drained

1 small onion, sliced thinly

1 garlic clove, crushed

1 tablespoon lemon juice

2 tablespoons low-fat natural yogurt

1 tablespoon chopped fresh
   coriander (optional)

1 Little Gem lettuce

salt and freshly ground black pepper

**1** Flake the tuna. Mix the chick-peas, tuna and onion in a bowl.

**2** In a small jug or dish, mix the garlic, lemon juice, yogurt, coriander, if using, and seasoning. Pour the dressing over the chickpeas and toss together.

**3** Break the lettuce into individual leaves and arrange round the edge of the bowl, like the petals of a flower.

**VARIATION:** Chicory could be used instead of lettuce and the salad could be served in individual bowls.

# BAKED POTATO WITH BLUE CHEESE AND PEAR

*Serves 1* ♦ *Preparation time 5 minutes* ♦ *Cooking time 1 hour 10 minutes* ♦
*Freezing recommended*

*There are more ideas for baked potato fillings next month. Jacket potatoes make a good light meal in winter and, if you have a microwave oven, they can be ready in minutes.*

Calories per serving: 265
Points per serving: 7
Ⓥ if using vegetarian cheese

1 baking potato (see page 193)

30 g (1 oz) half-fat blue cheese

1 ripe pear, peeled, cored and
   chopped

½ teaspoon ground cloves
   (optional)

salt and freshly ground black pepper

**1**  Preheat the oven to Gas Mark 7/220°C/425°F.

**2**  Slit the potato skin round the 'equator' and bake directly on the oven rack for 1 hour.

**3**  Meanwhile, mash the cheese in a basin with the chopped pear and ground cloves, if using.

**4**  When the potato is cooked, carefully split it in half and spoon out the cooked potato, mashing it with the cheese and pear. Season to taste. Scoop the lot back into the potato shells.

**5**  Grill until golden brown on top and serve at once.

# PORK AND RICE STIR-FRY

*Serves 4* ♦ *Preparation time 10 minutes* ♦ *Cooking time 50 minutes* ♦ *Freezing recommended*
*This makes a little meat go a long way. Mixed wild and long-grain rice is available in packets.*

Calories per serving: 320
Points per serving: 5
Total Points per recipe: 20

240 g (8 oz) mixed long-grain and
   wild rice

1 tablespoon vegetable oil

1 pork steak, trimmed of visible fat
   and cut in strips

2 garlic cloves, sliced

2 leeks, cleaned and sliced

120 g (4 oz) brussels sprouts,
   trimmed and quartered

1 green-skinned apple, cored and
   sliced

salt and freshly ground black pepper

**1**  Cook the rice according to the packet instructions and drain well.

**2**  Heat the oil in a wok or frying-pan.

**3**  Stir-fry the pork and garlic for 1 minute.

**4**  Add the leeks, brussels sprouts and apple slices and stir-fry for 4 more minutes.

**5**  Add the drained rice and toss until piping hot.

**6**  Season to taste and serve immediately.

# GAMMON WITH LEMON AND THYME POLENTA

◆

*Serves 4 ◆ Preparation time 10 minutes ◆ Cooking time 15 minutes ◆ Freezing not recommended*
*Polenta is a basic starchy food often used in Italian cooking. Because it does not have much*
*flavour of its own, stronger tasting ingredients are often served with it or added to it.*

Calories per serving: 450
Points per serving: 5
Total Points per recipe: 20

*1 tablespoon olive oil*

*2 gammon slices, trimmed of fat*
  *and cut in strips*

*240 g (8 oz) broccoli, broken into*
  *tiny florets*

*375 g packet instant pre-cooked*
  *polenta*

*grated zest and juice of 1 lemon*

*1 tablespoon chopped fresh thyme or*
  *2 teaspoons dried*

*2 tablespoons grated parmesan*
  *cheese (optional)*

*salt and freshly ground black pepper*

**1**  Heat the oil in a wok or frying-pan and stir-fry the gammon strips and broccoli. Keep warm.

**2**  Boil 2 litres (3½ pints) of water with 1 teaspoon salt.

**3**  Add the polenta, stirring constantly for one minute, or until thickened.

**4**  Add the grated lemon zest and juice, with the thyme.

**5**  Season to taste and pour into four serving bowls. Top with the stir-fried gammon and broccoli and sprinkle with parmesan cheese, if using.

# CHICKEN PASTA LAYER

◆

*Serves 4 ◆ Preparation time 10 minutes ◆ Cooking time 25 minutes ◆ Freezing recommended*
*This colourful dish has flavours of the Caribbean. It can be made in individual*
*freezer dishes and enjoyed anytime.*

Calories per serving: 400
Points per serving: 4
Total Points per recipe: 16

*2 boneless, skinless chicken breasts,*
  *cut in strips*

*3 tablespoons light soy sauce*

*2 garlic cloves, crushed*

*2.5 cm (1-inch) piece of fresh root*
  *ginger, chopped*

*1 tablespoon chopped fresh thyme or*
  *1 teaspoon dried*

*½ teaspoon cayenne pepper*

*240 g (8 oz) frozen peas, thawed*

*1 red pepper, de-seeded and chopped*

*4 celery sticks, sliced*

*240 g (8 oz) pasta shapes, in three*
  *colours if possible*

*150 ml (¼ pint) chicken stock*

*2 tablespoons fresh breadcrumbs*
  *(see page 135)*

*60 g (2 oz) half-fat cheese, grated*

*salt and freshly ground black pepper*

**1**  Preheat the oven to Gas Mark 6/200°C/400°F.

**2**  Place the chicken in an ovenproof dish.

**3**  Mix together the soy sauce, garlic, ginger, thyme and cayenne pepper and pour over the chicken, turning to coat.

**4**  Add the peas, pepper and celery, cover with foil and bake for 15 minutes.

**5**  Meanwhile, cook the pasta according to the packet instructions. Drain well.

**6**  Stir the pasta and stock into the chicken and season well.

**7**  Mix together the breadcrumbs and cheese and spoon over the top.

**8**  Either continue to bake, or place under a preheated grill until the crust is golden brown.

### Kitchen Notes

Poultry carcass and ham bones can both be used to make stock for soups, casseroles and pasta bakes such as this one. Place the carcass or bones in a large pan and add plenty of water to cover. Add two quartered onions and two unpeeled carrots, cut in large chunks. Season well and add a 'bouquet garni' and a couple of bay leaves. (A bouquet garni is a bunch of mixed herbs which can be tied in a muslin parcel. Much more convenient are the sachets, like tea bags, which are found in the herb and spice section of your supermarket.) Bring to the boil and then reduce the heat and simmer for at least 1 hour. Remove the bones and scrape any meat back into the stock. Refrigerate overnight and skim off any fat before using. Use within 3 days or freeze once cooled.

◆

# DUCK WITH PANCAKES AND PLUM SAUCE

♦

*Serves 4 ♦ Preparation time 15 minutes ♦ Cooking time 1 hour ♦ Freezing recommended*
*Choose dark red plums for this sharp sauce, which also goes well with chicken and lamb.*
*It can be made well in advance and stored in clean jars. I've included a recipe for thin Chinese*
*pancakes that would go well with this dish and can also be prepared ahead. As duck is such a*
*fatty meat, you should remove as much fat as possible from the cooked duck before eating.*

Calories per serving: 385
Points per serving: 9
Total Points per recipe: 36

*4 duck portions, either quarters or*
*    breasts (sometimes called*
*    magrets)*
*salt and freshly ground black pepper*
*shredded cucumber and spring*
*    onions, to serve*

**FOR THE SAUCE:**
*1 cooking apple, peeled, cored and*
*    cut in chunks*
*480 g (1 lb) dark red plums*
*120 ml (4 fl oz) wine vinegar*
*1 red chilli, de-seeded and chopped*
*    (optional)*
*artificial sweetener, to taste*

**FOR THE PANCAKES:**
*120 g (4 oz) plain flour*
*150 ml (¼ pint) boiling water*
*1 teaspoon vegetable oil*

**1**  Preheat the oven to Gas Mark 8/230°C/450°F.

**2**  Prick and season the duck portions and then place on a rack over a baking tin and cook for 20 minutes. Remove the skin when cool enough to handle, shred the meat and keep warm.

**3**  To make the sauce, cook the apple with 4 tablespoons of water in a covered pan, until the apple collapses. Add the whole plums, the vinegar and the chilli, if using, bring to the boil and then simmer, covered for about 1 hour. Sieve to remove the stones and skins and add artificial sweetener to taste.

**4**  To make the pancakes, sieve the flour into a basin. Mix in the boiling water and oil and knead until you have a smooth dough.

**5**  Cut the dough into eight pieces and roll each into a thin circle, about 13 cm (5 inches) in diameter.

**6**  Heat a non-stick frying-pan and put two pancakes in the pan, one directly on top of the other.

**7**  When the underside is done, turn the sandwiched pancake over and cook the other side (one side of each pancake will not be browned). Cook the rest of the pancakes and keep covered with a damp tea towel until ready to serve.

**8**  Serve the duck shredded, to roll up in the pancakes with the plum sauce.

**VARIATION:** You can omit the pancakes and serve the duck portions with green peas, accompanied by the plum sauce. Adjust the Points as necessary.

PORK AND RICE STIR-FRY *(page 161)*
DUCK WITH PANCAKES AND PLUM SAUCE

# LENTILS WITH AUTUMN VEGETABLES

◆

*Serves 4 ◆ Preparation time 10 minutes ◆ Cooking time 40 minutes ◆ Freezing recommended*
*This spiced casserole has robust flavours, warm and comforting on days which hint that winter is*
*on its way. Serve with some lightly cooked green vegetables, such as cabbage or broccoli.*

Calories per serving: 285
Points per serving: 3½
Total Points per recipe: 14
ⓥ

*1 tablespoon oil*

*1 onion, chopped*

*2 garlic cloves, crushed*

*1 teaspoon chilli powder*

*1 teaspoon ground cumin*

*240 g (8 oz) piece of peeled and*
*de-seeded pumpkin, cubed*

*1 yellow pepper, de-seeded and*
*chopped*

*1 red pepper, de-seeded and*
*chopped*

*1 aubergine, cubed*

*400 g can of chopped tomatoes*

*600 ml (1 pint) vegetable stock*

*240 g (8 oz) green lentils*

*salt and freshly ground black pepper*

*a sprig of fresh parsley, to garnish*

**1**   Heat the oil in a large pan and gently cook the onion, garlic, chilli powder and cumin for 5 minutes.

**2**   Add the pumpkin, peppers and aubergine, with a little seasoning, and cook over a low heat for 5 minutes.

**3**   Add the remaining ingredients, cover and cook for 30 minutes, or until the lentils are tender. Season to taste.

**4**   Transfer to a serving dish and garnish with a sprig of parsley.

# SESAME MEATBALLS AND VEGETABLE NOODLES

◆

*Serves 4 ◆ Preparation time 10 minutes ◆ Cooking time 15 minutes ◆*
*Freezing recommended for the meatballs*
*These vegetables are sliced with a potato peeler to look like noodles. You could cook pasta noodles*
*to mix with them.*

Calories per serving: 210
Points per serving: 4
Total Points per recipe: 16

*240 g (8 oz) minced pork or beef*
  *(see page 63)*
*2 tablespoons fresh wholemeal*
  *breadcrumbs (see page 135)*
*1 egg, beaten*
*1 tablespoon light soy sauce*
*1 tablespoon sesame seeds*
*1 garlic clove, crushed*
*1 tablespoon vegetable oil*
*2 carrots, peeled*
*2 courgettes, topped and tailed*
*salt and freshly ground black pepper*

**1**   Mix together the first six ingredients and season well.

**2**   Using wet hands, shape the mixture into walnut-sized meatballs.

**3**   Heat the oil in a frying-pan and cook the meatballs over a medium heat, turning frequently so that they are cooked evenly. Remove with a slotted spoon and keep warm.

**4**   Using a potato peeler, peel the carrots and courgettes into wide ribbons.

**5**   Add these to the pan, with 2 tablespoons of water, and stir-fry for 5 minutes.

**6**   Put the vegetable noodles on a warm plate and spoon the meatballs on top.

# TROUT WITH HERB STUFFING

◆

*Serves 2 ◆ Preparation time 10 minutes ◆ Cooking time 15 minutes ◆ Freezing not recommended*
*Trout fillets are used in this recipe. I have tried it with whole trout, but it is much easier to eat a*
*modest portion of fillet – and no bones to mess with either.*

Calories per serving: 195
Points per serving: 3½
Total Points per recipe: 7

*2 × 120 g (4 oz) trout fillets*

*120 g (4 oz) very-low-fat fromage*
  *frais*

*2 tablespoons chopped fresh mixed*
  *herbs (e.g. parsley, dill, chives)*

*1 garlic clove, crushed*

*grated zest and juice of 1 lemon*

*1 teaspoon vegetable oil*

*salt and freshly ground black pepper*

**1**  Preheat the grill. Spread the fillets out and season well.

**2**  Mix together the fromage frais, herbs, garlic, lemon zest and half the juice, and spread over the fillets. Season again.

**3**  Fold the fillets in half, so that the stuffing is inside, and brush the outsides with oil.

**4**  Grill under a medium heat for 5 minutes on each side.

**5**  Serve with the remaining lemon juice sprinkled over.

TROUT WITH HERB STUFFING
WATERCRESS, CELERY AND RADISH SALAD *(page 160)*

# LAMB PILAFF

◆

*Serves 4 ◆ Preparation time 10 minutes ◆ Cooking time 30 minutes ◆ Freezing recommended*
*Boil-in-the-bag brown rice is the easiest variety to use in this recipe. Pre-cook the rice and this*
*pilaff will take only minutes to cook.*

Calories per serving: 310
Points per serving: 4½
Total Points per recipe: 18

*1 onion, chopped*

*2 garlic cloves, crushed*

*120 g (4 oz) chestnut mushrooms,*
  *wiped and sliced*

*2 carrots, sliced*

*450 ml (¾ pint) tomato juice*

*2 sachets of boil-in-the-bag brown*
  *rice, cooked*

*1 tablespoon chopped fresh*
  *rosemary or 1 teaspoon dried*

*180 g (6 oz) frozen peas*

*2 teaspoons olive oil*

*240 g (8 oz) lamb fillet, cut in thin*
  *strips*

*2 tablespoons wine vinegar*

*salt and freshly ground black pepper*

**1**  In a large pan, cook the onion, garlic, mushrooms and carrots with the tomato juice for 5 minutes, until the onion is soft.

**2**  Add the cooked rice, rosemary and peas and simmer for 5 more minutes, adding a little water, if necessary.

**3**  Meanwhile, heat the oil in a frying-pan and stir-fry the lamb for 3 minutes, until sealed all over. Transfer to the rice mixture and stir in.

**4**  Spoon the vinegar into the frying-pan and allow it to bubble; scrape up all the meaty residue and stir it in with the lamb.

**5**  Season to taste and serve.

# BANANA BREAD

◆

*Makes a 480 g (1 lb) loaf (about 8 slices)* ◆
*Preparation time 10 minutes* ◆ *Cooking time 1 hour* ◆ *Freezing recommended*
*Use very ripe bananas in this recipe. The bread is best wrapped in greaseproof paper and stored
in an airtight tin for 1 day before slicing.*

Calories per slice: 170
Points per slice: 3
Total Points per recipe: 24

*½ teaspoon vegetable oil*

*120 g (4 oz) white or wholemeal
self-raising flour*

*½ teaspoon ground mixed spice*

*60 g (2 oz) polyunsaturated
margarine*

*90 g (3 oz) raisins*

*240 g (8 oz) peeled bananas*

*1 egg, beaten*

*½ tablespoon clear honey*

**1**  Preheat the oven to Gas Mark 4/180°C/350°F.

**2**  Brush a 480 g (1 lb) loaf tin with the oil.

**3**  Mix the flour and spice in a bowl and rub in the margarine.
Stir in the raisins.

**4**  Mash the bananas with the egg and honey. Pour them into the flour
and mix until blended together.

**5**  Spoon into the loaf tin and bake on the middle shelf for 1 hour, until
golden brown and firm.

**6**  Leave in the tin to rest for 10 minutes before turning out on to
a cooling rack.

# PEARS WITH BLACKBERRY SAUCE

◆

*Serves 2* ◆ *Preparation time 10 minutes* ◆ *Cooking time 15 minutes.*
*Freezing recommended for the sauce only*
*These two flavours marry well together. The dish is equally good hot or cold.*

Calories per serving: 90
Points per serving: 1½
Total Points per recipe: 3

*2 pears, peeled and left whole*

*1 lemon*

*1 cinnamon stick*

*120 g (4 oz) blackberries*

*1 teaspoon arrowroot*

*artificial sweetener, to taste*

**1**  Put the pears in a saucepan with a few strips of lemon zest
(use a potato peeler), 1 tablespoon of lemon juice, the cinnamon stick,
3 blackberries and just enough water to come half-way up the pears.
The blackberries will give the pears a delicate pink colour.

**2**  Bring to the boil and then simmer for 10 minutes.

**3**  Remove the pears, using a draining spoon. Discard the lemon zest and
cinnamon. Reserve 3 tablespoons of the poaching liquid in the pan.

**4**  Add the blackberries to the pan. Blend in the arrowroot and bring to
the boil, crushing the fruit occasionally. Remove from the heat and
sweeten to taste. Serve the pears on dessert plates, with the sauce around
them.

# November

White fish is at its best in the winter months and can be really succulent if cooked carefully. It contains only a trace of fat and so is an ideal food. Try it grilled and served with herbs, or use it in the Fish Pie (page 184).

Beef and pork are also good this month, but be sure to trim away all the visible fat before eating – be like Jack Sprat! Mince is the most popular way of buying meat of all sorts, so check the Tip Box on page 63 for how to choose and cook it.

The green leafy vegetables are all good right now, although it is said that brussels sprouts are at their best after the first frost.

Cranberries are appearing in the shops now and, although they are associated with Christmas cooking, these brilliant sharp red berries can be used in a variety of baking, puddings and savoury dishes. Bananas are also good and go so well with cranberries – try the dessert recipe on page 187. Easy-peel citrus fruits – like satsumas and mandarins – in season from this month through to January, also blend well with cranberries and make a refreshing start to the day or a delightfully simple dessert.

RABBIT AND PRUNE CASSEROLE *(page 180)*
STUFFED BAKED POTATO WITH BROCCOLI AND MUSHROOM *(page 175)*
STEWED CRANBERRIES AND BANANAS *(page 187)*

# DRIED FRUIT COMPOTE

◆

*Serves 4* ◆ *Preparation time 5 minutes + 1 hour steeping* ◆ *Cooking time 25 minutes*
*Freezing not recommended*
*This method of cooking dried fruit can be used for prunes, apricots, pears, peaches or apple rings*
*on their own. Serve it with yogurt or very-low-fat fromage frais.*

Calories per serving: 130
Points per serving: 2½
Total Points per recipe: 10

*2 Earl Grey tea bags*
*2 star anise or 1 teaspoon Chinese*
  *five-spice powder*
*250 g packet of dried fruit salad*

**1**   Pour 600 ml (1 pint) of boiling water over the tea bags and spice. Leave to infuse for 5 minutes.

**2**   Discard the tea bags and pour the tea over the dried fruit in a saucepan. Leave to soak for 1 hour.

**3**   Bring to the boil and then simmer for 20–25 minutes.

**4**   Serve either hot or cold.

*Slim Tips*
A tub of low-fat natural yogurt is a very
useful ingredient to have on hand.
You can mix it with your favourite
seasonal fruits to create a quick, tasty
and healthy low-Point snack at
any time of day.

◆

# STUFFED BAKED POTATOES

◆

*Serves 2 ◆ Preparation time 10 minutes ◆ Cooking time 1 hour ◆ Freezing recommended*
*Baked potatoes are quick to microwave but lack the crisp skin of oven-baked ones. Here are three*
*recipes for toppings which can be prepared while the potato is baking, whichever method you use.*

*2 baking potatoes (see page 193)*

*1 teaspoon vegetable oil*

*4 tablespoons skimmed milk*

*salt and freshly ground black pepper*

**1**  Scrub the potatoes and cut a line on the skin around the middle of each.

**2**  Bake at Gas Mark 7/220°C/425°F for 1 hour, or in the microwave according to the manufacturer's instructions.

**3**  Cut the potatoes in half and scoop out the cooked flesh. Mash with the oil, milk and seasoning and put back into the potato shells.

**4**  Spoon on a topping and grill to brown and crisp the cheese.

**FOR THE PIZZA TOPPING:**

Calories per serving: 115
Points per serving: 5
Ⓥ

*200 g can of chopped tomatoes*

*1 onion, chopped*

*1 garlic clove, crushed*

*½ green pepper, de-seeded and*
*  chopped*

*60 g (2 oz) half-fat mozzarella*
*  cheese, grated*

*salt and freshly ground black*
*  pepper*

Combine the tomatoes, onion, garlic and pepper in a pan and cook for 10 minutes. Season to taste. Spoon on to the baked potatoes and sprinkle with the cheese.

**FOR THE BROCCOLI AND**

**MUSHROOM TOPPING:**

Calories per serving: 140
Points per serving: 5½
Ⓥ

*1 teaspoon vegetable oil*

*240 g (8 oz) broccoli florets*

*120 g (4 oz) chestnut*
*  mushrooms, sliced*

*1 teaspoon soy sauce*

*2 tablespoons low-fat natural*
*  yogurt*

*60 g (2 oz) half-fat mozzarella*
*  cheese, grated*

*salt and freshly ground black*
*  pepper*

Heat the oil and stir-fry the broccoli and mushrooms for 5 minutes; add the soy sauce. Pour the yogurt over the potatoes and top with the vegetables. Season and sprinkle with the cheese.

**FOR THE BOLOGNESE**

**TOPPING:**

Calories per serving: 205
Points per serving: 6½

*120 g (4 oz) extra-lean minced beef*

*1 onion, chopped*

*1 garlic clove, crushed*

*2 tablespoons tomato purée*

*½ teaspoon dried mixed herbs*

*60 g (2 oz) half-fat mozzarella*
*  cheese, grated*

*salt and freshly ground black*
*  pepper*

Stir-fry the first five ingredients together over a medium heat, until the meat is cooked. Spoon over the potatoes, season and sprinkle with the cheese.

# SAUSAGE LOAF AND CURRIED BEANS

♦

*Serves 4 ♦ Preparation time 10 minutes ♦ Cooking time 15 minutes ♦*
*Freezing recommended for the loaf*
*This is a healthier variation on garlic bread, which all the family will enjoy.*

Calories per serving: 300
Points per serving: 5
Total Points per recipe: 20

*240 g (8 oz) half-fat cocktail or*
*  chipolata sausages*
*1 small french stick*
*1 onion, chopped finely*
*1 tablespoon brown sauce*
*1 teaspoon dried mixed herbs*
*420 g can of curried beans*

**1**  Preheat the oven to Gas Mark 7/220°C/425°F.

**2**  If using chipolata sausages, cut them in half before placing on a baking sheet in the oven. Bake for 5 minutes.

**3**  Meanwhile, cut the french stick almost through to the crust with the same number of cuts as you have sausage pieces.

**4**  Mix together the onion, brown sauce and herbs and put a spoonful in each cut.

**5**  Insert a sausage in each cut, and then wrap the whole loaf in kitchen foil and bake for 15 minutes.

**6**  Meanwhile, heat the curried beans. This can be done in the oven while the sausage loaf is cooking.

**7**  Carefully unwrap the loaf and cut into slices. Serve with the beans on the side.

# LEEK AND RICE SALAD

♦

*Serves 2 ♦ Preparation time 10 minutes ♦ Cooking time 20 minutes ♦ Freezing not recommended*
*When I want to rustle up a quick salad for lunch, I look to see what is in the fridge. In winter*
*there are always leeks – they have such a distinctive flavour and are surprisingly good raw.*

Calories per serving: 265
Points per serving: 2½
Total Points per recipe: 5
Ⓥ

*1 sachet of brown or white boil-in-*
*  the-bag rice*
*2 slender leeks, cleaned and sliced*
*1 red onion, chopped*
*2 tablespoons chopped fresh parsley*
*150 g tub of low-fat natural yogurt*
*grated zest and juice of 1 lemon*
*salt and freshly ground black pepper*
*½ teaspoon paprika, to garnish*

**1**  Cook the rice according to the packet instructions. Rinse, drain and place in a serving bowl.

**2**  Add the leeks, onion and parsley to the rice and stir together.

**3**  Mix together the yogurt, lemon zest and juice with seasoning to taste.

**4**  Pour over the salad and toss well. Serve sprinkled with paprika.

**VARIATION:** If you want to add an extra dimension to this salad, a can of drained sardines could be added. Each sardine will be 1 Point.

ITALIAN AUBERGINE *(page 178)*
SAUSAGE LOAF AND CURRIED BEANS

# HEARTY POTATO AND PAPRIKA SOUP

*Serves 4 ◆ Preparation time 10 minutes ◆ Cooking time 30 minutes ◆ Freezing not recommended*
*This South American-inspired soup is thick and satisfying.*

Calories per serving: 180
Points per serving: 2
Total Points per recipe: 8

1 tablespoon vegetable oil

1 onion, chopped

1 teaspoon paprika

480 g (1 lb) potatoes, peeled and cut
   into 2.5 cm (1-inch) cubes

900 ml (1¹/₂ pints) vegetable stock

150 ml (¹/₄ pint) skimmed milk

198 g can of sweetcorn

salt and freshly ground black pepper

**1** Heat the oil in a large pan and gently fry the onion with the paprika, for 5 minutes.

**2** Add the potatoes and stock, bring to the boil, and then cover and simmer for 25–30 minutes, when the potatoes should begin to fall apart.

**3** Add the milk and sweetcorn and heat through.

**4** Season to taste and serve at once.

**COOK'S TIP:** Use King Edward potatoes if you can find them.

# ITALIAN AUBERGINE

*Serves 1 ◆ Preparation time 10 minutes + 30 minutes salting ◆ Cooking time 25 minutes ◆*
*Freezing not recommended*
*This is much easier than stuffed aubergines. Salting the aubergine before cooking takes out some of the moisture, so that only a very little oil is needed. Serve with hot crusty bread.*

Calories per serving: 255
Points per serving: 2

1 aubergine, halved lengthways

1 courgette, cut in slices

2 garlic cloves, sliced thinly

227 g can of chopped tomatoes

6 stoned black olives, halved

1 teaspoon dried marjoram

2 teaspoons olive oil

salt and freshly ground black pepper

2 teaspoons grated parmesan cheese

**1** Score the flesh of the aubergine halves in a criss-cross fashion and sprinkle the cut surface with salt. Leave for 30 minutes.

**2** Combine the courgette, garlic, tomatoes, olives and marjoram in a pan, bring to the boil and simmer for 5 minutes. Season to taste and keep warm. Preheat the grill to medium.

**3** Rinse the aubergines and pat dry with kitchen paper.

**4** Rub the olive oil into the cut surfaces and grill for about 10 minutes on each side.

**5** Put the aubergines in a serving dish and spoon the topping over. Sprinkle with the parmesan cheese and serve.

# MUSHROOM AND SWEET POTATO FRITTATA

◆

*Serves 4* ◆ *Preparation time 10 minutes* ◆ *Cooking time 25 minutes* ◆
*Freezing not recommended*

*Sweet potatoes are delicious, and just as easy to cook as ordinary potatoes. This frittata is similar to a Spanish omelette, and makes a good light meal on an autumn day.*

Calories per serving: 205
Points per serving: 3½
Total Points per recipe: 14

240 g (8 oz) sweet potatoes

1 tablespoon olive oil

120 g (4 oz) field or flat
   mushrooms, sliced

1 garlic clove, crushed

1 tablespoon chopped fresh parsley

6 eggs, beaten

salt and freshly ground black pepper

**1**   Boil the sweet potatoes in lightly salted water for 20 minutes. Alternatively, prick the skins with a fork and cook in the microwave for 4 minutes on HIGH (100%).

**2**   Carefully peel off the skins and discard. Cut the potatoes into bite-sized pieces.

**3**   Heat the oil in a frying-pan and add the sweet potatoes, mushrooms and garlic. Fry for about 5 minutes, stirring occasionally.

**4**   Beat the parsley into the eggs and season well. Pour over the potatoes and mushrooms and cook over a low heat for 8 minutes. Preheat the grill.

**5**   When set and golden underneath, grill to cook the top of the frittata.

**6**   Turn out on to a warm plate and cut in wedges to serve.

# RABBIT AND PRUNE CASSEROLE

◆

*Serves 4 ◆ Preparation time 10 minutes ◆ Cooking time 1 hour ◆ Freezing recommended*
*Although this takes some time to cook, it can be left without any attention – and the smell of a*
*casserole cooking is very comforting in winter. Rabbit is a tasty low-fat meat, but you can use*
*skinless chicken portions if you prefer. Serve this with green vegetables and mashed potatoes.*

Calories per serving: 270
Points per serving: 5½
Total Points per recipe: 22

*4 rabbit portions, or 360 g (12 oz)*
  *boneless rabbit, cubed*

*1 tablespoon plain flour, seasoned*

*2 tablespoons olive oil*

*1 onion, chopped*

*2 celery sticks, sliced*

*4 tablespoons red wine vinegar*

*240 ml (8 fl oz) red wine*

*300 ml (½ pint) chicken stock*

*2 tablespoons tomato purée*

*2 teaspoons dried mixed herbs*

*12 ready-to-eat prunes*

*salt and freshly ground black pepper*

**1**  Preheat the oven to Gas Mark 4/180°C/350°F.

**2**  Rinse the rabbit and pat dry. Toss in seasoned flour to coat.

**3**  Heat the oil in a shallow pan and fry the onion, celery and rabbit until browned, turning regularly.

**4**  Add the remaining ingredients and bring to the boil, stirring constantly.

**5**  Transfer to an ovenproof casserole, cover and cook in the centre of the oven for 1 hour.

*Kitchen Notes*
Always choose cooking oils which are high in polyunsaturates and mono-unsaturates. Sunflower, safflower, groundnut and corn oils are all good for cooking, while olive oil, with its distinctive fruity flavour, is best for dressings and cooking Mediterranean-style food. A blend of sunflower and olive oil combines the best qualities of each. Use speciality oils, like sesame, hazelnut or walnut, sparingly, as they are expensive, and strong in flavour. Remember that all oils are high in Points, so however healthy your choice is, you should use the minimum amount necessary.
◆

# PORK STIR-FRY

◆

*Serves 4* ◆ *Preparation time 10 minutes* ◆ *Cooking time 15 minutes* ◆
*Freezing not recommended*
*The chillies in this stir-fry will warm you when the winter winds blow. The flavour is Chinese*
*in character and the dish has a thickened sauce to add extra moisture.*
*Serve with boiled rice noodles or fragrant rice.*

Calories per serving: 135
Points per serving: 2½
Total Points per recipe: 10

*1 tablespoon vegetable oil*
*240 g (8 oz) pork fillet, cut in*
  *thin strips*
*2.5 cm (1-inch) piece of fresh root*
  *ginger, chopped finely*
*2 garlic cloves, crushed*
*1 red chilli, de-seeded and shredded*
*1 green pepper, de-seeded and cut*
  *in thin strips*
*240 g (8 oz) bean sprouts*
*2 teaspoons cornflour*
*120 ml (4 fl oz) chicken stock*
*1 tablespoon light soy sauce*
*1 tablespoon dry sherry*
*½ teaspoon Tabasco sauce*
  *(optional)*
*salt and freshly ground black pepper*
*4 spring onions, sliced, to garnish*

**1** Heat the oil in a wok or deep frying-pan and stir-fry the pork strips until crisp. Remove from the wok and keep hot.

**2** Add the ginger, garlic and chilli and stir-fry for 3 minutes.

**3** Add the pepper and bean sprouts and stir-fry for 5 more minutes.

**4** Blend the cornflour with the stock, soy sauce, sherry and Tabasco sauce, if using. Add to the wok and stir until thickened.

**5** Return the pork to the wok, heat through and season to taste.

**6** Transfer to a warm serving dish and garnish with the spring onions.

# PEARL BARLEY AND PRAWNS

◆

*Serves 4* ◆ *Preparation time 10 minutes* ◆ *Cooking time 40 minutes* ◆
*Freezing recommended without prawns*
*If you think pearl barley is only for scotch broth or a winter casserole, then think again.*
*This recipe shows why pearl barley is fast becoming a trendy ingredient. Best of all, pearl barley is*
*a starchy food with lots of fibre and no fat and, since it's cheap, you can afford to be a little more*
*adventurous with the other ingredients.*

Calories per serving: 260
Points per serving: 3½
Total Points per recipe: 14

*1 tablespoon olive oil*

*1 onion, chopped*

*1 garlic clove, sliced*

*120 g (4 oz) pearl barley*

*900 ml (1½ pints) hot chicken stock*

*240 g (8 oz) peeled cooked prawns*

*1 tablespoon chopped fresh parsley*

*200 g tub of Quark*

*salt and freshly ground black pepper*

**1**   Heat the oil in a pan and gently cook the onion and garlic for 5 minutes, until soft but not browned.

**2**   Stir in the pearl barley and add the stock.

**3**   Bring to the boil and then reduce to a simmer and cook for 30–45 minutes, stirring occasionally.

**4**   Once the barley has absorbed most of the stock, add the prawns, parsley and Quark, and stir well. Season to taste.

**5**   Heat through for 5 minutes and then serve in a warm bowl.

# FISH PIE

♦

*Serves 4 ♦ Preparation time 10 minutes ♦ Cooking time 30 minutes ♦ Freezing recommended*
*Any white fish can be used for this – smoked fish would give it an extra-special flavour.*

Calories per serving: 210
Points per serving: 3½
Total Points per recipe: 14

*480 g (1 lb) cod or haddock fillet,*
*    skinned*
*300 ml (½ pint) skimmed milk*
*2 tablespoons cornflour*
*2 tablespoons chopped fresh parsley*
*1 tablespoon tomato purée*
*2 tomatoes, sliced*
*480 g (1 lb) potatoes, boiled and*
*    mashed with skimmed milk*
*salt and freshly ground black pepper*

**1**  Place the fish on a covered plate with 4 tablespoons of the milk, cover and steam for 15 minutes, until the flesh is firm and opaque.

**2**  Drain the milk from the fish and blend it with the cornflour.

**3**  Heat the remaining milk in a saucepan and stir in the cornflour paste. Cook, stirring constantly, until thickened.

**4**  Add the parsley and tomato purée and season to taste.

**5**  Flake the fish and combine gently with the sauce. Pour into the bottom of a pie dish or individual foil dishes.

**6**  Arrange the tomatoes over the top. Season again. Preheat the grill to medium.

**7**  Season the mashed potato and spread over the top. Rough up the surface using a fork.

**8**  Grill for 10 minutes, until golden and crisp on top and hot right through.

# CHICKEN AND PEPPER STIR-FRY

♦

*Serves 4 ♦ Preparation time 10 minutes ♦ Cooking time 30 minutes ♦ Freezing recommended*
*Jalfrezi is the Indian name for this chicken and pepper stir-fry flavoured with curry. This would*
*be lovely served with plain boiled rice and a tomato and coriander salad.*

Calories per serving: 270
Points per serving: 4
Total Points per recipe: 16

*1 tablespoon vegetable oil*
*1 onion, chopped*
*2 garlic cloves, crushed*
*4 skinless, boneless chicken breasts*
*    or thighs, cut in strips*
*2 tablespoons curry paste*
*1 green pepper, de-seeded and sliced*
*1 red pepper, de-seeded and sliced*
*200 g can of chopped tomatoes*
*salt and freshly ground black pepper*

**1**  Heat the oil in a wok or large frying-pan.

**2**  Cook the onion and garlic until just beginning to brown.

**3**  Add the chicken and stir-fry until sealed.

**4**  Cook for 15 minutes. Stir in the curry paste, peppers and canned tomatoes. Stir-fry for 10 more minutes and then season to taste, transfer to a serving bowl and eat at once.

# PARSNIP CANNELLONI

◆

*Serves 4 ◆ Preparation time 10 minutes ◆ Cooking time 30 minutes ◆*
*Freezing recommended before the sauce is added*
*If you can't find cannelloni tubes, use lasagne sheets. Soften them in boiling water for about*
*5 minutes and then drain well. Put the filling on one end of the lasagne sheet and roll up*
*before placing in the ovenproof dish.*

Calories per serving: 265
Points per serving: 3
Total Points per recipe: 12

*240 g (8 oz) parsnips, peeled and*
*  grated*
*1 onion, chopped finely*
*1 garlic clove, crushed*
*grated zest and juice of 1 lemon*
*1 teaspoon grated nutmeg*
*12 cannelloni tubes*

**FOR THE SAUCE:**

*1 tablespoon cornflour*
*300 ml (½ pint) skimmed milk*
*1 teaspoon prepared mustard*
*120 g (4 oz) half-fat cheese, grated*
*1 tablespoon dried breadcrumbs*
*  (see page 135)*
*salt and freshly ground black pepper*

**1**   Preheat the oven to Gas Mark 6/200°C/400°F.

**2**   Mix the grated parsnips with the onion and garlic. Stir in the lemon zest and juice and the nutmeg. Season well.

**3**   Spoon the mixture into the cannelloni tubes and lay them in an ovenproof dish or divide between 4 individual gratin dishes.

**4**   Blend the cornflour with the milk and mustard in a small pan. Bring to the boil and cook, stirring frequently, until thickened.

**5**   Remove from the heat and stir in all but 2 tablespoons of the grated cheese. Season to taste and pour the sauce over the cannelloni.

**6**   Mix the remaining cheese with the breadcrumbs and scatter over the top.

**7**   Bake for 20 minutes, covering the top with foil if it browns too quickly.

# APPLE MOUSSE

◆

*Serves 4 ◆ Preparation time 10 minutes ◆ Cooking time 10 minutes ◆ Freezing not recommended*
*This light apple dessert makes a refreshing end to any meal. You could also make it with ripe*
*pears, plums, damsons or dried apricots. Serve with a few ratafia biscuits, if you like.*

Calories per serving: 60
Points per serving: ½
Total Points per recipe: 2

*480 g (1 lb) cooking apples, peeled,*
  *cored and quartered*
*4 cloves (optional)*
*grated zest and juice of 1 lemon*
*artificial sweetener, to taste*
*1 egg white*
*1 red-skinned dessert apple*

**1**  Put the apple quarters into a pan with the cloves, if using, lemon zest, all but 1 tablespoon of the lemon juice and 1 tablespoon of water.

**2**  Bring to the boil and then cover and simmer for 5–10 minutes, until the apple is pulpy.

**3**  Beat well with a wooden spoon until smooth, remove the cloves and sweeten to taste. Leave to cool.

**4**  Whisk the egg white until stiff and fold into the apple purée.

**5**  Spoon into a serving bowl or individual dishes.

**6**  Quarter and core the apple. Slice and toss in the remaining lemon juice, to prevent it from turning brown. Arrange the slices on the apple mousse.

# STEWED CRANBERRIES AND BANANAS

♦

*Serves 2 ♦ Preparation time 5 minutes ♦ Cooking time 10 minutes ♦ Freezing recommended*
*The cranberry season begins this month. Their brilliant red colour and sharp flavour*
*complement bananas and make a warming dessert. This dish can also be eaten chilled,*
*and goes well with vanilla fromage frais.*

Calories per serving: 150
Points per serving: 3
Total Points per recipe: 6

*240 g (8 oz) cranberries*

*150 ml (¼ pint) unsweetened*
*orange juice*

*1 teaspoon ground cinnamon*

*2 bananas*

*artificial sweetener, to taste*

**1**  Rinse the cranberries and place in a saucepan with the orange juice and cinnamon.

**2**  Bring to the boil and then reduce to a simmer and cook for 8 minutes.

**3**  Peel and slice the bananas and add them to the pan. Simmer for 2 minutes. Sweeten to taste.

**4**  Transfer to a serving bowl or two individual dishes.

*Winter*

◆

# MENU PLAN

## MONDAY

**BREAKFAST**
1 small glass fruit juice:
½ Point
porridge made with
150 ml (¼ pint) skimmed
milk and granular artificial
sweetener: 2 Points

◆

**LUNCH**
2 slices low-Calorie bread:
1 Point
1 teaspoon low-fat spread:
½ Point
1 small can (300 g)
Weight Watchers from
Heinz Tomato Soup:
1 Point
2 satsumas: ½ Point

◆

**DINNER**
*Herring with Mustard
Topping (page 31):*
8 Points
3 scoops mashed potato:
3 Points
leeks and broccoli:
0 Points
1 tablespoon broad beans:
½ Point

─────
**MILK**
450 ml (¾ pint) skimmed
milk: 1½ Points
**TREAT**
1 small pot ready-to-eat
jelly: 1½ Points

## TUESDAY

**BREAKFAST**
1 medium bowl
cornflakes: 1½ Points
150 ml (¼ pint) skimmed
milk: ½ Point
1 small banana: 1 Point

◆

**LUNCH**
1 small glass fruit juice:
½ Point
1 slice toast: 1 Point
1 teaspoon low-fat spread:
½ Point
1 small can (205 g) Weight
Watchers from Heinz
Baked Beans: 1½ Points
salad of tomato, onion and
cucumber with fat-free
salad dressing: 0 Points

◆

**DINNER**
*Sizzling Beef Strips
(page 21):* 3½ Points
1 large portion rice:
4½ Points
grilled tomatoes: 0 Points
1 small tub low-fat natural
yogurt: 1½ Points

─────
**MILK**
150 ml (¼ pint) skimmed
milk: ½ Point
**TREAT**
1 choc ice: 3½ Points

## WEDNESDAY

**BREAKFAST**
1 slice toast: 1 Point
2 teaspoons low-fat
spread: 1 Point
1 heaped teaspoon jam or
marmalade: ½ Point

◆

**LUNCH**
*Seafood Pizza (page 199):*
4½ Points
*Chicory Salad (page 13):*
½ Point
1 apple: ½ Point

◆

**DINNER**
1 lamb chump chop,
grilled: 3½ Points
2 scoops mashed potato:
2 Points
leeks, carrots and cabbage:
0 Points
*Florida Flan (page 37):*
2½ Points

─────
**MILK**
600 ml (1 pint) skimmed
milk: 2 Points
**TREAT**
2 custard creams: 2 Points

| THURSDAY | FRIDAY | SATURDAY | SUNDAY |
|---|---|---|---|
| BREAKFAST | BREAKFAST | BREAKFAST | BREAKFAST |
| ¹/₂ grapefruit with granular artificial sweetener: ¹/₂ Point | *Fruited Porridge (page 10)*: 6¹/₂ Points | 1 egg scrambled with a little milk and butter: 3 Points | ¹/₂ grapefruit with granular artificial sweetener: ¹/₂ Point |
| 2 *Bacon and Potato Scones (page 193)*: 3 Points | ◆ | 1 slice toast: 1 Point | 1 slice bread: 1 Point |
| grilled tomatoes: 0 Points | LUNCH | 1 teaspoon low-fat spread: ¹/₂ Point | 1 teaspoon Marmite: 0 Points |
| ◆ | 1 medium baked potato: 2¹/₂ Points | 1 small glass fruit juice: ¹/₂ Point | ◆ |
| LUNCH | 1 tablespoon grated parmesan cheese: 1¹/₂ Points | ◆ | LUNCH |
| 1 medium pitta: 2¹/₂ Points | ¹/₂ small tub reduced-Calorie coleslaw: 1 Point | LUNCH | *Cod with Crumble Topping (page 14)*: 3 Points |
| 1 small can (100 g) tuna in brine: 1 Point | green salad with fat-free salad dressing: 0 Points | 1 small tub (110 g) diet cottage cheese: 1¹/₂ Points | 3 scoops mashed potato: 3 Points |
| salad of tomato, lettuce and onion with 2 tablespoons Weight Watchers from Heinz 1000 Island Salad Dressing: ¹/₂ Point | 2 kiwi fruits: 2 Points | salad of tomatoes and watercress with 2 tablespoons Weight Watchers from Heinz low-fat Blue Cheese Dressing: ¹/₂ Point | 1 small bunch grapes: 1 Point |
| ◆ | ◆ | 1 medium banana: 1¹/₂ Points | ◆ |
| DINNER | DINNER | ◆ | DINNER |
| 1 medium grilled chicken breast: 3 Points | 1 small glass fruit juice: ¹/₂ Point | DINNER | *Paprika Chicken (page 17)*: 3¹/₂ Points |
| 2 small roast potatoes: 3 Points | *Winter Vegetable Hot-Pot (page 34)*: 4 Points | *Lamb and Potato Curry with Raita (page 201)*: 6¹/₂ Points | 1 large portion rice: 4¹/₂ Points |
| brussels sprouts and carrots: 0 Points | | Weight Watchers from Heinz Dolcetta Ice Cream Dessert (100 ml): 2 Points | courgettes and carrots: 0 Points |
| 2 tablespoons peas: 1 Point | | | 1 small tub low-fat natural yogurt: 1¹/₂ Points |
| gravy made with 1 teaspoon gravy granules: ¹/₂ Point | | | |
| 1 small tub low-fat natural yogurt: 1¹/₂ Points | | | |

| | | | MILK |
|---|---|---|---|
| | | | 300 ml (¹/₂ pint) skimmed milk: 1 Point |
| MILK | | | TREAT |
| 300 ml (¹/₂ pint) skimmed milk: 1 Point | MILK | MILK | 1 small can (300 g) Weight Watchers from Heinz Chicken Noodle Soup: ¹/₂ Point |
| TREAT | 450 ml (³/₄ pint) skimmed milk: 1¹/₂ Points | 600 ml (1 pint) skimmed milk: 2 Points | 2 satsumas: ¹/₂ Point |
| 1 small banana: 1 Point | TREAT | TREAT | |
| 1 tablespoon dessert topping: 1¹/₂ Points | 1 tube Weight Watchers Fruities: ¹/₂ Point | 1 small glass wine: 1 Point | |

# December

This must be the most difficult month for healthy eating, dominated as it is by Christmas food in all its excess. Because friends and family expect everyone to eat well, it seems churlish to refuse. One or two hints which may help are to avoid between-meal and pre-meal snacks, like salted nuts and crisps. If you are desperate, make a bee-line for the fruit bowl, or keep a box of vegetable strips (see page 12) in the refrigerator.

Whenever you have the opportunity, eat winter vegetables on their own to balance against the Christmas excess. Celery is particularly good, and it is said that it takes more Calories to crunch and digest celery than there are in it! It certainly is a refreshing snack to nibble on. Broccoli and red cabbage are tasty and colourful and boiled beetroot can be eaten hot in a milky sauce, which it turns a bright shocking pink. Try it cold in a salad tossed in a fat-free dressing or vinegar. Turkey is a naturally low-fat meat and, like ham or pork, if the skin and any visible fat are removed, it is a very healthy choice. Try to use up leftover Christmas turkey in recipes like the Turkey Lasagne (page 203), instead of having it in the refrigerator waiting to be nibbled away.

SCRAMBLED EGG AND SMOKED SALMON *(page 192)*
BACON AND POTATO SCONES *(page 193)*
SPICED RED CABBAGE *(page 194)*
APPLE AND MINCEMEAT CRUNCH *(page 205)*

# SCRAMBLED EGG AND SMOKED SALMON

◆

*Serves 2 ◆ Preparation time 5 minutes ◆ Cooking time 5 minutes ◆ Freezing not recommended*
*For many years it has been the custom in our house to have this dish for breakfast on Christmas*
*Day. It is an excellent dish to enjoy at any time of the year as a special celebration light meal.*
*Buy smoked salmon trimmings, which are less expensive than the whole slices.*

Calories per serving: 265
Points per serving: 5
Total Points per recipe: 10

*2 slices of wholemeal bread*

*120 g (4 oz) smoked salmon*
  *trimmings*

*2 eggs*

*2 tablespoons skimmed milk*

*4 teaspoons low-fat spread*

*salt and freshly ground black pepper*

**1**  Toast the bread on both sides and keep warm.

**2**  Cut the salmon into bite-sized pieces

**3**  Beat together the eggs and milk and season well.

**4**  Heat the spread in a non-stick pan.

**5**  Add the beaten eggs and cook, stirring gently with a wooden spatula.

**6**  When just beginning to set at the edges, add the salmon and continue to stir until creamy and set.

**7**  Divide the egg between the toasts and serve immediately.

**COOK'S NOTE:** I think that a non-stick saucepan is essential for making scrambled eggs. One of the worst kitchen jobs, in my opinion, is washing up a scrambled egg pan which is not non-stick.

# BACON AND POTATO SCONES

◆

*Makes 8 wedges* ◆ *Preparation time 10 minutes* ◆ *Cooking time 30 minutes* ◆
*Freezing recommended*

*Potato scones can be bought ready-made, but the recipe below has a tasty breakfast ingredient
added and, as these can be frozen and cooked quickly, they are just as convenient.
These could be served with grilled tomatoes.*

Calories per wedge: 90
Points per wedge: 1½
Total Points per recipe: 12

*480 g (1 lb) maincrop potatoes,
    peeled and quartered (see below)*

*60 g (2 oz) plain flour*

*a little skimmed milk, to mix*

*60 g (2 oz) lean bacon or cooked
    ham, chopped finely*

*1 tablespoon chopped fresh parsley*

*oil, for brushing*

*salt and freshly ground black pepper*

**1**  Boil the potatoes in lightly salted water for 20 minutes, or until soft.

**2**  Drain and mash the potatoes with the flour and only enough milk
to leave it a stiff consistency.

**3**  Add the bacon or ham and parsley and mix well. Season to taste.

**4**  Brush the base of a frying-pan with oil and press the mixture evenly
over the pan. Cut into 8 wedges.

**5**  Heat the pan and cook the scones for 5 minutes; then turn carefully
and cook the other side.

*Kitchen Notes*

Choose the right potato for the job.
Most pre-packed potatoes found in
supermarkets give guidelines as to their
suitability for various cooking methods:
e.g. roasting, baking or boiling for
salads. In general, the 'old' or maincrop
potatoes have a high starch content,
and thus will be floury when cooked.
They are good for mashing or baking.
'New' potatoes are more suited for
boiling, especially in their skins, and
work well in salads. Growing climates
can change the character of
a potato, and so, during a very dry
season, not only will potatoes be
smaller, but they will not mash
as easily. At one time, potatoes were
only sold as 'white', 'red' or 'new', but
now you will find upwards of fifteen
varieties in any large supermarket, so
you can pick your own favourites.

◆

# SPICED RED CABBAGE

◆

*Serves 4 ◆ Preparation time 10 minutes ◆ Cooking time 30 minutes ◆ Freezing recommended*
*Red cabbage is not only a very pretty vegetable, it is also good natured! Although this dish*
*will be ready in 30 minutes, it can cook for longer and, if left to go cold and eaten the next day,*
*it is even more delicious. Remember that an acidic ingredient, like vinegar or lemon juice, is*
*needed to keep the colour red. If you boil cabbage on its own, it will go blue.*

Calories per serving: 85
Points per serving: 1
Total Points per recipe: 4

1 tablespoon vegetable oil

1 onion, chopped

1 garlic clove, sliced

480 g (1 lb) red cabbage, quartered
    and shredded finely, with stem
    removed

1 cooking apple, peeled, cored and
    quartered

1 tablespoon red wine vinegar or
    lemon juice

1 teaspoon ground mixed spice

¼ teaspoon grated nutmeg

150 ml (¼ pint) vegetable stock

salt and freshly ground black pepper

**1** Heat the oil and cook the onion and garlic gently until soft but not browned.

**2** Add the cabbage and the remaining ingredients.

**3** Stir well, bring to the boil and then simmer for 30 minutes or more.

**4** Adjust the seasoning to taste.

# BOMBAY POTATOES

♦

*Serves 4 ♦ Preparation time 10 minutes ♦ Cooking time 20 minutes ♦ Freezing recommended*
*These potatoes could be served as a side vegetable or, as I have suggested here, on a crisp papad,*
*an Indian 'crisp' that is grilled and not fried like a poppadom.*

Calories per serving: 180
Points per serving: 2
Total Points per recipe: 8

480 g (1 lb) potatoes, peeled

1 tablespoon vegetable oil

1 onion, chopped

2 garlic cloves, sliced

2 tablespoons curry powder

1 tablespoon wholegrain mustard
 (optional)

salt and freshly ground black pepper

4 papads, to serve

**1** Cut the potatoes into 2.5 cm (1-inch) chunks.

**2** Heat the oil in a saucepan and fry the onion and garlic until just beginning to brown.

**3** Stir in the curry powder and mustard, if using, with 2 tablespoons of water.

**4** Add the potatoes to the pan and toss to cover with the curry.

**5** Add another 150 ml (¼ pint) water, bring to the boil and then simmer for 20 minutes, or until the potatoes are tender. Season to taste.

**6** Grill the papads on both sides and then spoon the potatoes on top.

# BROCCOLI STIR-FRY

♦

*Serves 2 ♦ Preparation time 10 minutes ♦ Cooking time 8 minutes ♦ Freezing not recommended*

Calories per serving: 200
Points per serving: 1½
Total Points per recipe: 3

1 tablespoon vegetable oil

2 garlic cloves, sliced

2.5 cm (1-inch) piece of fresh root
 ginger

360 g (12 oz) broccoli, cut in florets

240 g (8 oz) brussels sprouts,
 trimmed and halved

1 red pepper, de-seeded and sliced

1 red chilli, de-seeded and sliced

2 spring onions, sliced

salt and freshly ground black pepper

**1** Heat the oil in a wok or large frying-pan and add the garlic and ginger. Stir-fry until sizzling.

**2** Add the broccoli, sprouts, red pepper and chilli and stir-fry for 5–8 minutes.

**3** Season and transfer to a warmed serving dish. Sprinkle with spring onions and serve hot.

COOK'S NOTE: This would be ideal served with cold turkey.

# POTATO AND CELERIAC PURÉE

◆

*Serves 4 ◆ Preparation time 10 minutes ◆ Cooking time 30 minutes ◆ Freezing recommended*
*Celeriac has a lovely celery-like flavour. It can be eaten raw in a salad, or boiled and mashed, or*
*roasted. If you prefer, you could make a celeriac purée on its own. This is great with roast poultry.*

Calories per serving: 160
Points per serving: 2
Total Points per recipe: 8

*480 g (1 lb) celeriac, peeled thickly*
*and cubed*
*480 g (1 lb) potatoes, peeled*
*and cubed*
*250 g tub of Quark*
*skimmed milk, to mix*
*salt and freshly ground black pepper*

**1**  Cook the celeriac and potatoes together in lightly salted boiling water for 20 minutes, until soft.

**2**  Drain and mash together well over a low heat, beating in the Quark.

**3**  If necessary, add a little skimmed milk to make a soft consistency.

**4**  Season to taste and serve hot.

# GREEK BEAN SALAD

◆

*Serves 4 ◆ Preparation time 10 minutes ◆ Freezing not recommended.*
*This salad will go well with any cold poultry you might have left over from Christmas dinner.*
*Use canned beans unless you are cooking for large numbers.*

Calories per serving: 80
Points per serving: 1
Total Points per recipe: 4

*215 g can of butter beans, rinsed*
*and drained*
*¹/₂ × 432 g can of cannellini beans,*
*rinsed and drained*
*1 onion, sliced thinly*
*1 garlic clove, sliced thinly*
*2 tablespoons lemon juice*
*2 teaspoons olive oil*
*a few sprigs of fresh flat-leaf parsley*
*salt and freshly ground black pepper*

**1**  Mix together the beans, onion and garlic in a bowl.

**2**  Whisk the lemon juice and oil together with some seasoning, and pour over the beans.

**3**  Garnish with the parsley sprigs and serve chilled.

GAMMON WITH MUSTARD AND LIME *(page 198)*
POTATO AND CELERIAC PURÉE
GREEK BEAN SALAD

# GAMMON WITH MUSTARD AND LIME

◆

*Serves 2 ◆ Preparation time 5 minutes + 1 hour marinating ◆*
*Freezing recommended for the cooked gammon only*
*It's likely that you will have some ham left over from Christmas to make this simple dish.*
*Make sure that all the visible fat is trimmed from the cooked ham.*

Calories per serving: 60
Points per serving: 5½
Total Points per recipe: 11

*2 slices of cooked gammon or ham,*
  *trimmed of fat*
*2 tablespoons very-low-fat fromage*
  *frais*
*1 teaspoon wholegrain or Dijon*
  *mustard*
*grated zest and juice of 1 lime*
*salt and freshly ground black pepper*
*watercress or young spinach, to*
  *garnish*

**1**  Put the ham slices on a serving dish.

**2**  Mix together the fromage frais, mustard, lime juice and seasoning.

**3**  Spoon over the gammon and put in a cool place to marinate for
1 hour.

**4**  Garnish the edges of the plate with watercress or spinach leaves and
scatter the grated lime zest on top.

# SEAFOOD PIZZA

◆

*Serves 1 ◆ Preparation time 5 minutes ◆ Cooking time 10 minutes ◆ Freezing recommended*
*Mini pizza bases are just right for a quick hot lunch. Freeze the rest of the packet*
*and defrost as needed.*

Calories per serving: 260
Points per serving: 4½

1 mini pizza base
200 g can of chopped tomatoes
1 garlic clove, sliced
1 teaspoon dried mixed herbs
60 g (2 oz) peeled prawns or other
  prepared shellfish
6 stoned olives (optional)
30 g (1 oz) half-fat mozzarella
  cheese, grated
salt and freshly ground black pepper

**1** Preheat the oven according to the packet instructions for the
pizza base.

**2** Heat the tomatoes, garlic and herbs in a pan, simmering until slightly
thickened. Season well.

**3** Put the pizza base on a baking sheet and spread the tomato mixture
over the base. Arrange the shellfish, olives, if using, and cheese on top.

**4** Bake according to the packet instructions.

# LAMB AND POTATO CURRY WITH RAITA

◆

*Serves 2 ◆ Preparation time 10 minutes ◆ Cooking time 30 minutes ◆ Freezing not recommended*
*Choose vegetables which are in season for this curry. In the summer, use french beans and*
*courgettes or spinach. Curry powder and pastes can be bought in different strengths, so buy one*
*to suit your taste buds. Fillet of lamb is a tender cut and does not need long cooking. The raita*
*can be served with any curry; it has a cooling effect against spices.*

Calories per serving: 450
Points per serving: 6½
Total Points per recipe: 13

*2 tablespoons vegetable oil*

*120 g (4 oz) neck lamb fillet, cubed*

*1 potato, peeled and cubed*

*1 onion, chopped*

*2 garlic cloves,*

*1 tablespoon curry powder or paste*

*240 g (8 oz) cabbage, shredded*

*120 ml (4 fl oz) vegetable stock*

*salt and freshly ground black pepper*

**FOR THE RAITA:**

*150 g tub of low-fat natural yogurt*

*5 cm (2-inch) piece of cucumber,*
   *cubed*

*a pinch of paprika*

*salt*

**1**   Heat the oil in a pan and fry the lamb, potato, onion, garlic and curry powder or paste for 5 minutes.

**2**   Add the cabbage and vegetable stock.

**3**   Bring to the boil, season and then simmer until the lamb and potatoes are tender.

**4**   Meanwhile, to make the raita, mix the yogurt and cucumber together, season to taste and sprinkle with paprika.

**5**   Serve the curry with the raita.

### Slim Tips

Indian food is perhaps the most
popular exotic cuisine eaten in this
country. In addition to the restaurants
and take-aways, the range of ready-
meals, chutneys and breads in
supermarkets is enormous. For healthy
eating, choose simple tandoori grills,
which are usually served with a salad.
If you have enough Points left for rice,
opt for plain boiled rice. If not, have a
cucumber raita (cucumber and yogurt)
with your main course. In general,
vegetarian dishes contain less fat and
Calories than meat dishes.

◆

BOMBAY POTATOES *(page 195)*
LAMB AND POTATO CURRY WITH RAITA

# LEEK AND LENTIL PILAFF

◆

*Serves 4 ◆ Preparation time 5 minutes ◆ Cooking time 25 minutes ◆ Freezing not recommended*
*It is difficult to say how much stock the lentils and rice will absorb, so be prepared to add some*
*more if necessary. This dish could also be served as a side dish, in which case it will serve six.*

Calories per serving: 285
Points per serving: 3½
Total Points per recipe: 14
Ⓥ

480 g (1 lb) leeks, cleaned, trimmed
  and cut in 5 mm (¼-inch) slices
750 ml (1¼ pint) vegetable stock
2 teaspoons ground coriander
1 teaspoon ground cumin
180 g (6 oz) long-grain rice
120 g (4 oz) red lentils
2 garlic cloves, crushed
salt and freshly ground black pepper

1  Put the leeks in a large pan or flameproof casserole with 4 tablespoons of stock and the spices.

2  Cover and cook slowly for 5 minutes, until the leeks have softened.

3  Stir in the rice, lentils, garlic and the remaining stock. Bring to the boil.

4  Cover and simmer for 15–20 minutes, stirring occasionally and adding more stock, if necessary.

5  Season to taste and serve hot.

# GREEN VEGETABLE BAKE

◆

*Serves 4 ◆ Preparation time 10 minutes ◆ Cooking time 30 minutes ◆ Freezing recommended*
*Choose a selection from the many green winter vegetables available – brussels sprouts, broccoli,*
*leeks, kale, spinach, green peppers and patty-pan squash are all good.*

Calories per serving: 205
Points per serving: 2
Total Points per recipe: 8
Ⓥ

2 onions, chopped
2 garlic cloves, sliced
960 g (2 lb) mixed green vegetables
1 tablespoon chopped fresh thyme
150 ml (¼ pint) vegetable stock
120 g (4 oz) fresh brown
  breadcrumbs (see page 135)
60 g (2 oz) half-fat cheese, grated
salt and freshly ground black pepper

1  Preheat the oven to Gas Mark 5/190°C/375°F.

2  Put the chopped onions and the garlic in the bottom of an ovenproof dish.

3  Prepare the green vegetables and shred or cut into bite-sized pieces.

4  Mix the greens with the onions, garlic and chopped thyme. Pour the stock over and season well.

5  Mix together the breadcrumbs and cheese and spoon over the top.

6  Bake for 30 minutes, covering with a piece of foil if the top browns too quickly.

# TURKEY LASAGNE

♦

*Serves 4 ♦ Preparation time 15 minutes ♦ Cooking time 1 hour ♦ Freezing recommended*
*A lasagne is an excellent way to use up Christmas leftovers, which are incorporated in*
*the meat and tomato sauce. Choose lasagne sheets which do not need pre-cooking.*
*Serve with a green salad.*

Calories per serving: 420
Points per serving: 6½
Total Points per recipe: 26

*1 onion, chopped*

*2 garlic cloves, crushed*

*400 g can of chopped tomatoes*

*1 teaspoon dried mixed herbs*

*240 g (8 oz) cooked lean turkey,*
   *chopped*

*480 g (1 lb) mixed cooked*
   *vegetables, preferably green*
   *leafy ones*

*4 tablespoons cornflour*

*300 ml (½ pint) skimmed milk*

*300 ml (½ pint) turkey or*
   *chicken stock*

*½ teaspoon grated nutmeg*

*240 g (8 oz) no-pre-cook lasagne*
   *sheets (6–8 sheets)*

*120 g (4 oz) half-fat cheese, grated*

*salt and freshly ground black pepper*

**1**   Put the onion, garlic and tomatoes in a non-stick saucepan with the herbs and seasoning. Bring to the boil and then simmer for 10 minutes.

**2**   Add the turkey and vegetables and cook for 10 minutes more.

**3**   Meanwhile, blend the cornflour with a little of the skimmed milk in a small pan.

**4**   Add the remaining milk, the stock and nutmeg, bring to the boil and cook, stirring constantly, for 5 minutes. Add a little more stock if the sauce gets too thick. Season to taste.

**5**   Preheat the oven to Gas Mark 6/200°C/400°F.

**6**   Assemble the lasagne in an ovenproof dish. Put half the meat sauce in the bottom of the dish, cover with half the lasagne sheets, and top with half the white sauce. Repeat the layers and top with the grated cheese.

**7**   Bake for 30 minutes, until golden brown. Allow to rest for 5–10 minutes before serving.

# WHITE CHOCOLATE VELVET

♦

*Serves 4 ♦ Preparation time 5 minutes + 30 minutes chilling ♦ Freezing not recommended*
*This is just the dessert for a white Christmas! It looks and tastes sinful, but appearances are*
*deceptive! Decorate the top with a festive garnish or sprinkle cocoa on top.*

Calories per serving: 240
Points per serving: 6½
Total Points per recipe: 26

Ⓥ

*150 g (5 oz) white chocolate*

*360 g (12 oz) very-low-fat fromage*
  *frais, at room temperature*

*1 teaspoon cocoa powder*

**1**  Melt the chocolate in a heatproof bowl over a pan of simmering water.

**2**  Blend the melted chocolate into the fromage frais and pour into four serving dishes.

**3**  Chill until set and dust with cocoa powder before serving.

# APPLE AND MINCEMEAT CRUNCH

◆

*Serves 4 ◆ Preparation time 10 minutes ◆ Cooking time 25 minutes ◆ Freezing recommended*
*This satisfying pudding will use up those annoying remains of mincemeat*
*left over from the mince pies.*

Calories per serving: 275
Points per serving: 5
Total Points per recipe: 20
Ⓥ if using vegetarian mincemeat

*480 g (1 lb) cooking apples, peeled,*
  *cored and sliced*
*2 tablespoons mincemeat*
*2 tablespoons water*
*1 tablespoon orange juice*
*60 g (2 oz) polyunsaturated*
  *margarine*
*120 g (4 oz) rolled oats*
*1 tablespoon granular artificial*
  *sweetener*

**1**   Preheat the oven to Gas Mark 5/190°C/375°F.

**2**   Combine the apple slices, mincemeat, water and orange juice in a pan and cook for 5 minutes. Pour into a pie dish.

**3**   Rub the margarine into the oats and spoon on top of the apple and mincemeat mixture.

**4**   Bake for 20 minutes, until golden brown, and sprinkle with artificial sweetener before serving.

**COOK'S NOTE:** For an even quicker pudding, leave off the crunch topping. Either way, a scoop of Weight Watchers vanilla ice-cream would be a delicious accompaniment.

**WEIGHT WATCHERS TIP:** To reduce the fat content of this pudding, chill the apple and mincemeat mixture after step 2 and skim the fat from the surface before reheating.